: **Issue

How Should One Cope with Death?

Elaine Minamide, *Book Editor*

Bruce Glassman, *Vice President*
Bonnie Szumski, *Publisher*
Helen Cothran, *Managing Editor*

GREENHAVEN PRESS
An imprint of Thomson Gale, a part of The Thomson Corporation

THOMSON
—————*—————™
GALE

Detroit • New York • San Francisco • San Diego • New Haven, Conn.
Waterville, Maine • London • Munich

LIBRARY OF CONGRESS CATALOGING-IN-PUBLICATION DATA

How should one cope with death? / Elaine Minamide, book editor.
   p. cm. — (At issue)
Includes bibliographical references and index.
ISBN 0-7377-2386-6 (lib. : alk. paper) — ISBN 0-7377-2387-4 (pbk. : alk. paper)
   1. Death. I. Minamide, Elaine. II. At issue (San Diego, Calif.)
BD444.H69 2006
155.9'37—dc22   2005046109

Printed in the United States of America

Contents

Introduction

When a person is born, we rejoice, and when they're married we jubilate, but when they die, we try to pretend that nothing happened.
—Margaret Mead, anthropologist

It has been estimated that approximately 57 million people die every year. Divide that number by 365 days in the year and you get this figure: Approximately 155,000 people die in the world every *day.* Based on these numbers, it would be logical to assume that the topic of death would be somewhat pedestrian. After all, not only is death an everyday occurrence, it is also an inevitable one: each of us, eventually, will die.

According to some experts, such an assumption would be wrong. Most people are not comfortable talking about death, let alone preparing for it. Discussing death has been compared to looking at the sun: we know it is there, but it is painful to stare directly into it. In her book *Handbook for Mortals: Guidance for People Facing Serious Illness*, physician Joanne Lynn writes, "Most of us do not plan for serious illness and death. And many of us feel that if we don't talk about bad things, they won't happen to us." J. Donald Schumacher, president and CEO of the National Hospice and Palliative Care Organization (NHPCO), notes that we live in a "death-defying society" and "broaching this subject is difficult for most of us." Trinity University professor of sociology Michael Kearl writes, "Americans are forgetting about how to learn to focus on dying as a human process, how to include the dying in their dialogues, and how to learn the lessons of their existence. Instead, the dying process now too often features silence or diversion."

Although conversations about death and dying are admittedly unpleasant, experts maintain that such conversations are essential. Fran Moreland Johns, author of *Dying Unafraid* and board president of Compassion in Dying, points out that "accidents, serious illness, or sudden injury can and do strike without warning, bringing people of all ages to the edge of death every day."

The truth and poignancy of this statement is graphically illustrated in the case of a forty-one-year-old Florida woman named Terri Schiavo, who died just about the time this book was being prepared for publication.

Terri Schiavo was twenty-six when she suffered severe brain damage during cardiac arrest. Subsequently diagnosed as being in a persistent vegetative state, Schiavo was kept alive by feeding tubes as her case wended its way through the legal system and her loved ones argued over custody and treatment. Her death in a Florida hospice followed nearly fifteen years of bitter personal and legal battles between Schiavo's parents, who believed there was a chance for their daughter's rehabilitation, and Schiavo's husband, Michael, who maintained that his wife would not have wanted to be kept alive through artificial means. Although Terri Schiavo had left nothing in writing about her wishes, Michael Schiavo based his claim on conversations said to have taken place when Terri was in her twenties.

The Schiavo case monopolized the news for weeks as world leaders, politicians, physicians, lawyers, and ethicists weighed in on such controversial issues as physician-assisted suicide and the right to die. Complicating the legal and ethical debate was the absence of any kind of formal, legal document (advance directive) from Terri Schiavo in which her end-of-life wishes were clearly expressed. Absent this document, Schiavo's life remained in limbo. Her fate ultimately rested in the hands of the courts, which eventually agreed with Michael Schiavo and ruled that the feeding tube keeping his wife alive could be removed. On March 31, 2005—thirteen days after the tube was removed—Terri Schiavo died.

Schiavo's death by court decree riveted a culture unaccustomed to talking about death. In the aftermath, conversations about death and dying seemed to be everywhere. In coffee shops and on talk radio, people argued and debated. Family members formerly uncomfortable discussing such a painful subject wrote, called, or e-mailed loved ones, pestering them to "get it in writing." In the weeks after Schiavo died, the NHPCO Web site reported that "tens of thousands, if not millions, of people have requested information on advance care planning." The Aging with Dignity Web site announced that requests for "Five Wishes"—a living will document that helps people explore legal, medical, emotional, and spiritual issues—increased from fifty per day to more than six thousand requests in a single day. "We've never seen anything that compares to the level of interest in the spring of 2005," Aging with Dignity president Paul Malley wrote in an update following Schiavo's death. "National media attention stirred an unprecedented interest in living wills around the country." No longer something to be mentioned in embarrassed, hushed whispers, suddenly it was ordinary to talk about death.

Some experts disagree about whether advance directives—which can include living wills, medical powers of attorney, and other documents that specify medical-treatment wishes—address all relevant legal and medical end-of-life issues. "There are major differences between the types of advance directives," observes Rita Marker, executive director of the International Task Force on Euthanasia and Assisted Suicide. For this reason, Marker recommends appointing a durable power of attorney, someone who can speak on one's behalf in the event of mental incapacity. However, most experts do agree that it's better to have something in writing than nothing. The International Task Force on Euthanasia and Assisted Suicide says that people are at risk unless "[they] have taken the simple but necessary step of signing an advance directive" if they are unable to make their own decisions.

If death is so common, why don't people want to talk about it, let alone actively prepare for it? Part of the answer could be that to mention the unmentionable somehow seems to invite its reality. Nevertheless, the statistics are clear: The mortality rate for all of us is 100 percent. In *At Issue: How Should One Cope with Death?* the reader is invited to "stare into the sun" and explore this difficult yet important subject.

1

American Culture Does Not Help the Dying Cope with Death

John Cloud et al.

John Cloud is a staff writer for Time *magazine. Reporters Wendy Cole, Maggie Sieger, Dan Cray, Greg Fulton, Anne Moffett, and Dick Thompson also contributed to this article.*

Most Americans do not plan well for death. Statistics indicate that even when people prepare advance directives, these documents are often ignored. Health professionals and academics believe there is a need for reform in the way Americans face death. Reform is especially needed in the area of pain management; too many patients die in horrible pain. There also needs to be better dialogue between doctors and dying patients, as well as better funding for competent end-of-life care and hospice. The most important reform, however, has to do with encouraging Americans to arrange better deaths for themselves.

Dying is one of the few events in life certain to occur—and yet one we are not likely to plan for. We will spend more time getting ready for two weeks away from work than we will for our last two weeks on earth. Consequently, says Frank Ostaceski, who runs a San Francisco home for the dying, "we have more preparation for how to operate our VCRs than we do for how to die."

But as [French actor and playwright Jean-Baptiste] Moliere

joked, "We die only once—and for so long!" So we should choose to die well. Too many of us don't. According to a new TIME/CNN poll, 7 out of 10 Americans say they want to die at home; instead, three-fourths die in medical institutions. More than a third of dying people spend at least 10 days in intensive-care units, where they often endure torturous (generally futile) attempts at a cure. Specialists say 95% of pain in terminally ill people can be mollified, but studies show that nearly half of Americans die in pain, surrounded and treated by strangers. A recent survey found that 3 out of 5 physicians treating dying patients had known them less than a week.

We plan assiduously for retirement. Yet about a third of Americans bankrupt their families in the process of dying. Sometimes they don't want all the IVs and monitors and bills yet suffer them anyway. Even in 1997, 30 years after the first living will was written in the U.S. to prevent overtreatment, 1 in 10 dying Americans said in a survey that his wishes were ignored. Too often, in the words of the Rev. George Caldwell, who ministers to the dying in Virginia, people die in "the final, tiny, helpless cosmos of a hospital bed."

Since 1975, when Karen Ann Quinlan's father went to the New Jersey courts to get her respirator turned off, the debate over dying in America has focused on a narrow question: Is there a right to die? But that struggle, so agonizing and dramatic, overshadows practical questions that will prove more important for most of us: How will we die, and can we die more comfortably?

> *Many cancer patients experience horrible pain near death.*

A group of reform-minded physicians, caregivers and academics hopes to change the way doctors approach dying. They want all of us to discuss it sooner. . . . "Our expectations as a culture for end-of-life care are too low," says Dr. Ira Byock, author of *Dying Well: Peace and Possibilities at the End of Life.* He thinks the assisted-suicide debate misses the point: "Doctors spend 12 minutes with you, even if you have a serious illness. So we only have a couple minutes to listen to your deepest fears, but we're going to give you the black pill?"

It may be a propitious moment for reform. Those who bore the baby boomers are nearing their end. Like everything else they have come across and disliked, boomers are taking note of the ways in which their parents are dying—and trying to do something about it. The growing movement to improve the way we die is the subject of [this essay]. These are the stories of people who have managed to die more comfortably, who have demanded better care from their doctors, who have talked about what's next with their families. If they are lucky, they have discovered how to cast some light over the shadow of death, in spite of a system that conspires against dying well.

> *Medical schools have only just begun to introduce curriculums in managing pain and other symptoms of the dying.*

You would think Bob Cummins would have had the most attentive health care as he neared the end of his battle with prostate cancer. The former lawyer was being treated in two of the best hospitals in New York City. He wasn't fabulously wealthy; he had devoted most of his time to producing jazz records, which aren't big moneymakers. But at age 69, Cummins had a nest egg.

Many cancer patients experience horrible pain near death, and even the best oncologists don't always know how to ease it. "I got the usual—'Load 'em with codeine'—and I couldn't focus across the room," Cummins recalled. The drugs sapped his will to do anything but stare at Knicks games. A friend who also has cancer phoned one day to ask if he had tried any new treatments. No. "It hit me," Cummins said later, weeping at the memory. "I had just given up."

He sought out a pain specialist and eventually found the department of pain medicine and palliative care at Beth Israel Medical Center in Manhattan, one of only a handful of such facilities in the U.S. Dr. Lauren Shaiova prescribed fentanyl, a stronger pain medication that made Cummins comfortable but not cloudy. Finally, his agony and fog lifted. "We call her our angel," said Nancy, Bob's wife, of Shaiova. But she was only practicing basic pain management, using readily available drugs. "Most docs just say, 'There's nothing more we can do,'" laments Shaiova. "I tell them, 'I can actively treat your pain.'"

Many doctors flinch at using controlled substances because of the nation's harsh antidrug laws. A 1998 survey of New York State physicians found that 71% chose a drug that did not require a triplicate form—necessary for dispensing many controlled substances such as fentanyl—even when the controlled drug was the appropriate treatment. Instead they regularly choose weaker medications because they fear legal scrutiny.

Many physicians are also erroneously worried that they will addict patients or even kill them. Last year [1999] Kathleen Foley, another New York City pain specialist, released a study showing that 40% of her fellow neurologists wrongly believed that using a dose of morphine big enough to control breathlessness would actually euthanize the patient. (In truth, there's no ceiling dose of morphine, as long as the patient is given time to adjust.)

Barbara Strong, 59, suffered because of such ignorance. Miami doctors refused the former nurse's pleas for medication when horrific cancer pain struck. After Strong rebelled and found a pain specialist, her regular doctor "went wacko. . . . He said I would become addicted." So Strong stayed with the oncologist; eventually her pain got so awful she could barely move. "I wanted to be dead," she says. As a Christian, Strong couldn't go through with actually *killing* herself. . . .

Instead, Strong dumped her doctor and called Dr. Pamela Sutton, the specialist who had helped her before. Soon she was back on the golf course. She could play until recently, when her condition slid. "I wouldn't be alive today if not for Pam Sutton," she says. Strong is fortunate to have sought help. Many don't, for a misguided reason: 82% of respondents in one study agreed with a pollster that "it is easy to become too reliant on pain medication." In fact, fewer than 1% of those treated with opioids become addicted.

Cummins, too, improved. He and his wife were able to meet the emotional challenges of terminal illness without the physical demands of agony. They listened to jazz; she offered spiritual guidance; they continued to decorate their East Harlem apartment with mosaics. "The quality of my life definitely improved," Cummins said, "and that goes hand in hand with prolonging it." Even his oncologist enthusiastically welcomed Shaiova's pain treatment. "He's happy about it," Cummins said. "He's a great doctor, but he's just not trained in pain management."

Most aren't. Medical schools have only just begun to introduce curriculums in managing pain and other symptoms of the dying. The subjects are difficult to teach because most professors don't know the material, and most textbooks say little about end-of-life care. It wasn't until 1997 that the American Medical Association began developing a continuing-education packet for doctors on the subject. The group that accredits hospitals began requiring them to implement pain-management plans only this year. "In the past few years, we have seen a sea change of improvements in the issue," says Foley, "but we've known how to do this since 1975."

> *Americans as a whole have a hard time discussing dying—even those who have planned for it.*

Managing pain better would allow patients more comfortable deaths, but it can't guarantee easier ones. "When it comes to dying, pain comes in many flavors," says Robert Wrenn, who recently retired after 24 years of teaching about the psychology of dying at the University of Arizona. "Spiritual pain, social pain, even the unfinished-business pain that asks, 'Why am I here?'" Only the creepy would say dying should be cause to rejoice, and only the idealistic would say the health-care system could change our attitudes about it. But Byock, author of *Dying Well*, notes that dying's place in our culture has changed before. Until recently, most people died at home, because doctors couldn't do much. "Since the era when antibiotics were invented and surgery began to be safe, in the '30s, the focus has become to combat disease. The subject of the patient has too often been lost," says Byock.

As dying was medicalized, it was removed from our lives—to the ICU and the funeral home—both fairly new institutions if you consider how long people have been dying. Dislodged by modernity, dying became a taboo, slightly gross subject for polite conversation. Physicians and the families of their patients began to see death as a defeat, not an inevitable culmination. "We need education," says Dr. Kerry Cranmer of the American Medical Directors Association. "Instead surgeons get together when a patient dies to find out who screwed up."

Which isn't to blame doctors alone. Americans as a whole have a hard time discussing dying—even those who have planned for it. According to the TIME/CNN poll, 55% of those over 65 now have an *"advance directive,"* a legal document that lays out what sort of care they want before death. This number has never been higher. But only 6% of those worked with a doctor to write the document; other polls have shown that very few people even tell their doctors they have *advance directives.* In addition, a study found that although many Americans legally designate someone else to make medical decisions after they are unable to, 30% of those who have been designated don't know they have been picked. Even our faith leaders, the people many of us seek out for guidance near the end, have a hard time giving it. "The truth is, clergy are frequently not comfortable with end-of-life care," says Keith Meador, Duke University professor of theology and medicine. A report found that one-third of clergy members had no training to help dying people.

> **What she needed was a chance to discuss the reality of her impending death.**

The reformers hope to begin a new dialogue about dying, one that integrates its enlightening potential. Says Byock: "Dying people have the chance to say what matters most, renew spirituality, complete relationships. . . . It's not fun, not pretty, and I don't want to romanticize it, but, gee, it's not without some value." In a society that hides dying, however, it's often hard to see that value. Last year, retired New York psychologist Felice Gans, 72, was diagnosed with incurable pancreatic cancer. She was originally told she had two months, but she has lived more than a year. (Such imprecision is common. A University of Chicago study found recently that only 20% of physicians' predictions of survival were accurate.) So uncertainty colors Gans' life—will she be able to take a long-planned train trip this month through the Rockies? Many days bring "stark terror. . . . I sometimes wish that I had a belief system," she sobs. "Then I feel like I'm two years old, and I have no control. I spend part of every day mourning my own death."

And yet Gans, who never married, doesn't have anyone to help guide her. Though she likes her doctor as an oncologist, he is fairly brisk during their appointments, as HMO-era doctors must be. Even when she was first told she had a terminal illness, the doctor and staff gave little comfort. "They don't want you crying," Gans says. A nurse had two words for her: "Calm down." Eventually Gans found a support group, Gilda's Club, named for comedian Gilda Radner, who died of ovarian cancer. When Gans arrived for the first meeting, she saw that it was called a "wellness group." But what she needed was a chance to discuss the reality of her impending death—her frail appearance, the sheer mundanity of her days. "I'm not into talking about, 'Maybe they're going to find a drug for me,'" she explained.

So how do we fix these problems? The first step, say the reformers, is to change the way we think about the end. "It's not about death," says Joanne Lynn, director of the RAND Center to Improve Care of the Dying. "It's really about living with a disease that's going to kill you, about good living on the way to death. We spend as much time with our fatal illness as we spend as toddlers."

Changing attitudes means getting more people to give up rescue medicine in favor of comfort care when the hope of a cure is minuscule. "For many people, it's easier to say, 'Whatever you say, Doc,' rather than spend two weeks thinking through your own death," says Lynn. "That's uncomfortable. But life is mostly about grandchildren and gardening, sunrises and eating chocolate. It's not about pills." Fine, but how do you eat a Hershey bar when you know it could be your last?

One solution is hospice, a kind of care for the dying that emphasizes comfort over cure. Hospice patients must forgo further curative and life-prolonging treatments, which means they usually leave the hospital. (A hospice can be a separate place, but usually the word refers to home care.) Doctors, social workers, art therapists and others manage physical pain and help patients navigate the emotional terrain of dying.

When John Wracian, 80, was first diagnosed with colon cancer last year, the former General Motors supervisor from Downey, Calif., underwent surgery. But when it didn't work, he accepted that chemotherapy probably wouldn't either. Instead, a hospice nurse checked on him and his wife Carol twice a week, as did a chaplain. "It's the best thing that came along," said John, who read several books a week and watched the Dodgers. "Nine days in the hospital [for surgery] was more than enough. Now I'm home, enjoying the life I have." He and

Carol didn't expend energy on frequent trips to doctors; instead, the couple focused on saying goodbye. "When the time comes and he's gone, I won't have to look back and say, 'I wish I would have said that,'" said Carol, recalling that her dad passed away without ever speaking with her mother about his dying. John Wracian died Sept. 2 [2000].

Hospice can also have more practical benefits. "We discuss whether they need a homemaker to wash dishes or read to the patient so his wife can get out because she's exhausted," says Margaret Clausen, president of the California Hospice Foundation. On average, hospice patients receive at least three hours a day more attention than nursing-home patients. And hospice is cheaper than traditional care. For example, at Balm of Gilead Center, a hospice in Birmingham, Ala., the average cost per patient per day is $720, in contrast to $3,180 for ICU patients.

> *On average, hospice patients receive at least three hours a day more attention than nursing-home patients.*

But hospice, which well-meaning clergy members imported to this country from Britain in the 1970s, ministers to only 17% of dying Americans. "The word hospice has toxic connotations," says Clausen. That's partly because Medicare starts a fatal clock ticking on hospice patients: it will reimburse for hospice only after two doctors certify that a patient has less than six months to live. But many doctors are reluctant to do so, especially for unpredictable diseases like heart failure. Some physicians also fear regulatory scrutiny, since the U.S. Health Care Financing Administration has actually ordered investigations of hospice patients who live longer than six months. Some fear that a short prognosis will be self-fulfilling, and many just don't like to tell someone he is dying. Hence the average length of stay in U.S. hospices is between two and three weeks, hardly enough time to take advantage of a hospice's supportive environment.

So long as it requires people to abandon hope of full recovery, hospice is unlikely to become a mainstream phenomenon. Most people want to fight, hang on, hope for a miracle. Recently, Cummins, the jazz producer, heard that he could qualify for a clinical trial. He knew the trial carried only a remote possibility of a cure, but he didn't want to give up. Even so, when he and Nancy totaled the cost of his pain medications—$2,250 a month—they were presented with a cruel choice: opt for hospice to save money, or go for the trial and keep paying for the drugs themselves (the Medicare hospice reimbursement includes prescriptions; Medicare generally doesn't). "So it's hospice vs. bankruptcy," said Cummins. He and Nancy chose hospice care. Bob died at home Aug. 17, [2000] before the trial began.

Other patients also face difficult choices because hospices don't usually offer pricey procedures such as dialysis, radiation or chemotherapy—even when designed merely to palliate symptoms. George Thielman, a retired printer from Chicago, didn't want to stop life-prolonging dialysis after a cancerous kidney was removed and the other began to fail. "Ultimately, he died in a nursing home, a place none of us wanted him to be," his daughter Betsy says. "We were always operating in crisis mode."

Another shortcoming of hospice is that not everyone can afford or wants to die at home. (Although a few hospitals have inpatient hospices and 30% of nursing homes now contract with hospice companies, 90% of hospice patients live at home.) Gans, the retired psychologist who lives alone in a Manhattan high-rise, is worried that she will need medical care at night. More generally, African Americans, Russian immigrants and others who have had less access to health care fear that doctors who recommend hospice are trying to get rid of them. "All people want to die with dignity, but the definition is different," says Dr. Annette Dula, who wrote a book on ethics in African-American medical care. "In the black population, people want aggressive, continuing treatment even if it means food tubes, pain, antibiotics and losing their savings. It's a sign of respect."

> *The most challenging reform may be to get patients to become their own advocates for better death.*

Designing a health-care system that would take into account every unique death would be impossible. But reformers say there are a few things the U.S. could do to improve how most of us die. First, insurance companies could reimburse more kinds of palliative care, which is cheaper than attempting a cure. "Insurance will routinely cover expensive chemo with a 5% chance of success but may not cover opioids for pain relief," says Foley, the pain specialist. "We are talking about a redistribution of money that we already spend." When Dr. Shaiova was caring for Cummins, she spent an hour with him one day explaining what hospice could do for him. "How do I describe to Medicare how I treated him that day?" she asked. Currently, many palliative-care and hospice programs rely on donations to stay afloat.

[In September, 2000], Congress will consider ways to increase the use of Medicare's hospice benefit.[1] [Iowa] Senator Charles Grassley, the Republican who chairs the Special Committee on Aging, wants to clarify Medicare's requirement of a six-month life expectancy as a guideline, not a hard rule. (Reformers hope Congress will formally declare it an average instead of a cap.) Senators Susan Collins [of Maine], a Republican, and Jay Rockefeller, a Democrat [from West Virginia], also plan to introduce a more general end-of-life health-insurance plan.

Next, more states could begin programs like one in Oregon that offers all patients a form stating their preferences on resuscitation, tube feedings and so on. That state has also benefited from two referendum campaigns on *assisted suicide*, which taught voters a great deal about the current shortcomings of end-of-life care. Today only about a third of Oregon residents die in institutions, in contrast to the 75% national average. As a state, Oregon spends the lowest amount on inpatient care in the final six months of life.

Cities can adopt some of the changes under way in Missoula, Mont., where a project called the Quality of Life's End is educating local doctors, lawyers, clergy members and students about what it means to die well. For example, both of Missoula's hospitals now treat pain as a fifth vital sign, ensuring that medical staff will take it seriously. Recently the project contacted Missoula's lawyers to begin teaching them to write better *advance directives*. And project volunteer Gary Stein incorporates end-of-life issues into the high school psychology course he teaches.

Graduate schools could also teach more about how we die, particularly medical and nursing schools as well as seminaries.

---

1. The Benefits Improvement Protection Act of 2000 (BIPA) was enacted and contained a 5 percent increase in Medicare Hospice Benefit (MHB) base payment rates.

Current managers of nursing homes and geriatric wards could inquire about the [American Medical Association's] course on end-of-life care and subscribe to the three-year-old *Journal of Palliative Medicine.* They can learn a lot from Veterans Affairs hospitals, many of which have made improvements in end-of-life treatment in the past five years.

Doctors could speak more openly with patients about prognosis and mention comfort care when a serious illness is first diagnosed—even as traditional treatments are explored. Then, if a cure isn't found, advises Dr. Fred Meyers, who chairs the department of internal medicine at the University of California at Davis, "be honest and say, 'I don't think I can cure you, but I'm not going to abandon you; you're going to get good consultation, we'll take care of your symptoms and take care of your family.'"

The most challenging reform may be to get patients to become their own advocates for better death. That would require frank talk about a somber subject. That's not an entirely unreasonable expectation, reformers contend. They point out that Americans successfully changed birth in the 1960s and '70s by getting fathers more involved and focusing more on mothers' well-being. Byock believes that the boomers, who demanded many of the changes in the way we come into the world, will be equally insistent on changing the way we leave. "The baby boomers are the most self-centered, arrogant, willing-to-try-new-things generation ever," says the 49-year-old, who drives a Saab. "They're going to bring the same collective raising of expectations to the care we give people who are living through the end of their lives."

2

Access to Physician-Assisted Suicide Can Help Patients Cope with Death

Marcia Angell

Marcia Angell is former editor in chief of the New England Journal of Medicine *and is senior lecturer at the Department of Social Medicine at Harvard Medical School.*

The Oregon Death with Dignity Act, a voter-approved initiative that made physician-assisted suicide legal in the state of Oregon, provides a way for people to die with dignity. Physician-assisted suicide gives terminally ill patients the option of dying peacefully, surrounded by their family and loved ones. Such an option was not available to the author's father, who died violently of a self-inflicted gunshot wound. Dying patients like the author's father and countless others nearing the end of their lives must have the opportunity to exercise the right to die with dignity. The Oregon Death with Dignity Act makes this possible.

[In 1997], people of Oregon voted overwhelmingly to permit physician-assisted suicide for terminally ill patients whose suffering cannot be relieved in any other way. Since then, about 20 Oregonians a year have chosen this option, and the law seems to be working exactly as intended.

But [former] Attorney General John Ashcroft has announced

he will prosecute Oregon physicians who help their patients in this way. Oregon is now seeking a permanent injunction to stop him.[1] Hearings in the case—*State of Oregon v. Ashcroft*—will begin soon. I have decided to tell the story of my father in an amicus brief in the case, because it illustrates what is at stake. Here is that story.

On March 15, 1988, my father, Lester W. Angell, then 81 years old, took a pistol from his bedside table and shot himself through the head. He died instantly. About seven years earlier he had been diagnosed with prostate cancer. For a few years, he did reasonably well with treatment.

> *He knew he had nothing to look forward to except further decline and a protracted death. Worst of all for him was the prospect of losing his independence.*

Four months before his death, however, the cancer began to spread throughout his body, and he required radiation for excruciating back pain. Although the pain was lessened, he suffered from nausea and vomiting as a result of the radiation and from side effects of his various medications. He knew he had nothing to look forward to except further decline and a protracted death. Worst of all for him was the prospect of losing his independence.

My father was a man of great dignity for whom independence was enormously important. He saw it as his responsibility to take care of his family, not the other way around. He had a successful career as a civil engineer, first with the Tennessee Valley Authority, then the Army Corps of Engineers and eventually as chief design engineer of the St. Lawrence Seaway. In World War II, despite being in his late thirties, he volunteered and served as a Seabee in the South Pacific. (He had a lot in common with the fictional Mr. Roberts.) He later became a lieutenant colonel in the Army Reserve. He was a lifelong conservative Re-

1. On May 26, 2004, the Ninth Circuit Court of Appeals ordered the Bush administration not to interfere with Oregon's assisted suicide law. On February 22, 2005, the Supreme Court agreed to hear the Bush administration's challenge to the nation's only right-to-die law. The high court is not likely to rule on this issue until 2006.

publican who believed in patriotism and the duties of citizenship. But he also believed in the right to self-determination. To my knowledge, he never suffered from depression.

His Lonely and Violent Death

At the time my father killed himself, he was living with my mother near Orlando, Fla. My mother was a housewife and had always been dependent on him. Now it was the other way around. The day before his death, he fell while walking to his bed from the bathroom. My mother was unable to lift him, so she called the emergency medical technicians. They lifted him to the bed and said they would return the next day to take him to the hospital to make certain he had not fractured a bone. I believe he decided to kill himself that night because he thought it might be his last chance to do it. He had always kept a pistol in his bedside table. Had he gone to the hospital the next day, he would have been without it, and might never again have had the option of ending his own life.

> *If physician-assisted suicide had been available to my father, as it is to the people of Oregon, I have no doubt he would have chosen a less violent and lonely death.*

My mother was sleeping in the next room and had to bear the shock of finding his body. If he had told her his intentions, she would have stopped him, as she later told me. So he did not tell her. Later, I could see from the trajectory of the bullet that he had turned in such a way that the bullet could not have gone through the wall and harmed her. I believe he had planned on the possibility of taking his own life for some time, since he had left his affairs in perfect order, including a long letter to my mother, with copies to my brother and me, instructing her on exactly what needed to be done. My father also did not tell me of his intentions, even though I am a physician and he confided in me about other aspects of his illness. Although I do not know for certain why he didn't tell me or ask for my help, I suspect he didn't want to compromise me in any way.

If physician-assisted suicide had been available to my father, as it is to the people of Oregon, I have no doubt he would have chosen a less violent and lonely death. My mother could have been brought around to accepting his decision, death could have been peaceful, and his family could have been with him. If he had known he had the option to get help in ending his life at any time in the future, he probably also would have chosen to live longer. That night would not have been his last chance.

My father's situation was hardly unique or even unusual. Many people with terminal illness face the same dilemma. It is not a choice between life and death. It is a choice between a slow, agonizing death and a quick, merciful one. Many people—not just my father—would choose the latter if they could. What was unusual about my father was not his choice but his courage and resolve in achieving it.

The Oregon Death with Dignity Act makes that choice much easier for patients and their families. But it does not preclude people from making a different choice. People who prefer a longer life to an easier death are not prevented from choosing that. It seems to me that Oregon has chosen a path that gives dying patients the opportunity to exercise the greatest possible self-determination with the full support of their families and communities. I cannot imagine why anyone would want to prevent that.

3

Access to Physician-Assisted Suicide Is Unnecessary

Joe Loconte

Joe Loconte is the William E. Simon Fellow in Religion and a Free Society at the Heritage Foundation, where he examines the role of religious belief in strengthening democracy and reforming civil society.

Lost in discussions about doctor-assisted suicide is the hospice alternative. Hospice programs, in existence since the 1970s, provide humane, compassionate care for the dying, often allowing people to die in homes rather than in hospitals. In spite of the prevalence of hospice programs in the United States, many terminally ill people either have never heard of the hospice option or enter hospice programs too late to benefit from their services. Those who do not know about hospice fear dying in pain and often advocate for physician-assisted suicide. However, hospice personnel concentrate on managing pain, and, more crucially, helping the terminally ill live as fully as possible until they die. With hospice care readily available, physician-assisted suicide is unnecessary.

In the deepening debate over assisted suicide, almost everyone agrees on a few troubling facts: Most people with terminal illnesses die in the sterile settings of hospitals or nursing homes, often in prolonged, uncontrolled pain; physicians typically fail to manage their patients' symptoms, adding mightily to their suffering; the wishes of patients are ignored as they are subjected to intrusive, often futile, medical interventions; and aggressive end-of-life care often bankrupts families that are already in crisis.

Too many people in America are dying a bad death.

The solution, some tell us, is physician-assisted suicide. Oregon has legalized the practice for the terminally ill. Michigan's Jack Kevorkian continues to help willing patients end their own lives. The prestigious *New England Journal of Medicine* has come out in favor of doctor-assisted death. Says Faye Girsh, the director of the Hemlock Society: "The only way to achieve a quick and painless and certain death is through medications that only a physician has access to."

This, we are told, is death with dignity. What we do not often hear is that there is another way to die—under the care of a specialized discipline of medicine that manages the pain of deadly diseases, keeps patients comfortable yet awake and alert, and surrounds the dying with emotional and spiritual support. Every year, roughly 450,000 people die in this way. They die in hospice.

The Alternative to Doctor-Assisted Suicide

"The vast majority of terminally ill patients can have freedom from pain and clarity of mind," says Martha Twaddle, a leading hospice physician and medical director at the hospice division of the Palliative CareCenter of the North Shore, in Evanston, Illinois. "Hospice care helps liberate patients from the afflictions of their symptoms so that they can truly live until they die."

The hospice concept rejects decisions to hasten death, but also extreme medical efforts to prolong life for the terminally ill. Rather, it aggressively treats the symptoms of disease—pain, fatigue, disorientation, depression—to ease the emotional suffering of those near death. It applies "palliative medicine," a team-based philosophy of caregiving that unites the medical know-how of doctors and nurses with the practical and emotional support of social workers, volunteer aides, and spiritual counselors. Because the goal of hospice is comfort, not cure, patients are usually treated at home, where most say they would prefer to die.

"Most people nowadays see two options: A mechanized, depersonalized, and painful death in a hospital or a swift death that rejects medical institutions and technology," says Nicholas

Christakis, an assistant professor of medicine and sociology at the University of Chicago. "It is a false choice. Hospice offers a way out of this dilemma."

If so, there remains a gauntlet of cultural roadblocks. Hospice is rarely mentioned in medical school curricula. Says Dale Smith, a former head of the American Academy of Hospice and Palliative Medicine, "Talk to any physician and he'll tell you he never got any training in ways to deal with patients at the end of life."

The result: Most terminally ill patients either never hear about the hospice option or enter a program on the brink of death. Though a recent Gallup Poll shows that nine out of 10 Americans would choose to die at home once they are diagnosed with a terminal disease, most spend their final days in hospitals or nursing homes.

And, too often, that's not a very good place to die. A four-year research project funded by the Robert Wood Johnson Foundation looked at more than 9,000 seriously ill patients in five major teaching hospitals. Considered one of the most important studies on medical care for the dying, it found that doctors routinely subject patients to futile treatment, ignore their specific instructions for care, and allow them to die in needless pain.

> *Most people nowadays see two options: A mechanized, depersonalized, and painful death in a hospital or a swift death that rejects medical institutions and technology. . . . Hospice offers a way out of this dilemma.*

"We are failing in our responsibility to provide humane care for people who are dying," says Ira Byock, a leading hospice physician and the author of *Dying Well*. George Annas, the director of the Law, Medicine and Ethics Program at Boston University, puts it even more starkly: "If dying patients want to retain some control over their dying process, they must get out of the hospital."

That's precisely the argument that hospice advocates have been making for the last 25 years. Hospice programs are, in fact, the only institution in the country with a record of compassionate, end-of-life care for people with incurable illnesses. The hospice movement, and the palliative approach to medicine it represents, could revolutionize America's culture of dying.

The Hospice Philosophy

Since the mid-1970s, hospice programs have grown from a mere handful to more than 2,500, available in nearly every community. At least 4,000 nurses are now nationally certified in hospice techniques. In Michigan—Kevorkian's home state— a statewide hospice program cares for 1,100 people a day, regardless of their ability to pay. The Robert Wood Johnson Foundation, a leading health-care philanthropy, has launched a $12-million initiative to improve care for the dying. And the American Medical Association, which did not even recognize hospice as a medical discipline until 1995, has made the training of physicians in end-of-life care one of its top priorities.

There is a conflict raging in America today over society's obligations to care for its most vulnerable. Says Charles von Gunten, a hospice specialist at Northwestern Memorial Hospital, in Chicago, "It is fundamentally an argument about the soul of medicine." One observer calls it a choice between hospice or hemlock—between a compassion that "suffers with" the dying, or one that eliminates suffering by eliminating the sufferer.

The modern hospice movement was founded by English physician Cicely Saunders, who, as a nurse in a London clinic, was aghast at the disregard for the emotional and spiritual suffering of patients near death. In 1967, she opened St. Christopher's Hospice, an in-patient facility drawing on spiritual and practical support from local congregations.

> *The hospice movement, and the palliative approach to medicine it represents, could revolutionize America's culture of dying.*

"She wanted to introduce a distinctly Christian vision to mainstream medicine," says Nigel Cameron, an expert in bioethics at Trinity International University, in Deerfield, Illinois. The staples of the hospice philosophy quickly emerged: at-home care; an interdisciplinary team of physicians, nurses, pharmacists, ministers, and social workers; and a heavy sprinkling of volunteers.

Saunders' vision got a boost from *On Death and Dying*, Elisabeth Kübler-Ross's book based on more than 500 interviews with dying patients. The study, in which the author pleaded for greater attention to the psychosocial aspects of dying, became an international bestseller. By 1974, the National Cancer Institute had begun funding hospices; the first, in Branford, Connecticut, was regarded as a national model of home care for the terminally ill. . . .

Case Study: John Brown's Death Wish

Hospice care usually begins where traditional medicine ends: when it becomes clear that a person's illness will not succumb to even the most heroic of medical therapies. "This is the toughest problem for doctors and families, the issue of letting go," says Alan Smookler, the Palliative Care-Center's assistant medical director. "There's a lot of technology out there—feeding tubes, antibiotics, oxygen, ventilators, dialysis—and the hardest problem is saying that these interventions are no longer beneficial."

Such was the case for John Brown, diagnosed with terminal cancer. Brown (not his real name) was treated with radiation and chemotherapy in a Washington, D.C.–area hospital. The treatments proved ineffective, and the pain from his cancer got worse. His wife convinced him to enter care at a local hospice program.

"His immediate request was that his wife call several friends, all of whom were hunters, and ask them to shoot him," says the Reverend Jeanne Brenneis, of the Hospice of Northern Virginia. "This was a man very used to being in control, and he was frightened of being helpless and in pain."

The hospice team concentrated first on relieving Brown's physical discomfort. His physician prescribed several pain-killing drugs, while a nurse watched for other symptoms. Within a couple of days, his pain was under control.

Though mostly bed-bound, Brown spent the next five months at home laboring as best he could at his favorite hobby: boat design. The hospice team set up a drafting board by his bedside so he could go on working. He finished one design and was halfway through another when he died.

He caught up on some other business as well: spending time with his wife and adult daughters and, after years of avoiding church, coming to terms with God. "He had time to reflect and think," Brenneis says, "and he grew a great deal emotionally and spiritually in that time."

The Need for Pain Management

Brown's story is no longer remarkable. Interviews with hospice caregivers uncover a singular experience: Once the pain and symptoms of an illness are under control, people rarely talk about taking their own lives. "Those requests go away with good palliative care," says von Gunten, who directs palliative education at Northwestern University Medical School. "I see this on a routine basis."

The Hospice of the Florida Suncoast, in operation since 1977, works mostly with retirees in Pinellas County. Now the largest community-based hospice in the country, it has about 1,200 patients under care on any given day. Programs extend to nearly all of the 100 or so nursing homes in the area. About 80 percent of all county residents with end-stage cancer find their way into its orbit of care.

The hospice team concentrated first on relieving [the patient's] physical discomfort. . . . Within a couple of days, his pain was under control.

Hospice president Mary Labyak says many people come in eager to hasten their own deaths, but almost always have a change of heart. Of the 50,000 patients who have died under the group's care, she says, perhaps six have committed suicide. "The public perception is that people are [choosing suicide] every day. But these are people in their own homes, they have the means, they have lots of medication, and they don't choose death."

Hardly anything creates a more frightening sense of chaos than unrelieved pain and suffering. "We know that severe pain greatly reduces people's ability to function," says Patricia Berry, the director of the Wisconsin Cancer Pain Initiative. "If we don't control symptoms, then people can't have quality of life, they can't choose what they want to do or what to think about."

By interrupting sleep, curbing appetite, and discouraging personal interactions, pain doesn't just aggravate a person's physical condition. It also leads, as a recent report by the Institute of Medicine puts it, to "depression and demoralization" of the sufferer. Says David English, the president of the Hospice of Northern Virginia, one of the nation's oldest programs, "You can't address the psychosocial issues of a person who is in pain."

Hospice has understood this connection between pain and overall well-being from the start. After conventional treatments fail, says Martha Twaddle, "you'll often hear doctors say 'there's nothing left to do.' There's a lot left to do. There is a lot of aggressive care that can be given to you to treat your symptoms."

> *Once the pain and symptoms of an illness are under control, people rarely talk about taking their own lives.*

Hardly anyone doubts that more energetic caregiving for the dying is in order. A 1990 report from the National Cancer Institute warned that "undertreatment of pain and other symptoms of cancer is a serious and neglected public health problem." The New York State Task Force on Life and the Law, in arguing against legalizing assisted suicide, cited the "pervasive failure of our health-care system to treat pain and diagnose and treat depression."

The best studies show that most doctors still undertreat pain and that most people with chronic and terminal illnesses experience needless suffering. A survey was taken [in 1995] of 1,177 U.S. physicians who had cared for more than 70,000 patients with cancer during the previous six months. Eighty-five percent said the majority of cancer patients with pain were undermedicated; nearly half of those surveyed rated their own pain management techniques as fair or very poor. . . .

The Need for Palliative Care

Not long ago oncology staff from Evanston Hospital, counseled in pain control techniques by Martha Twaddle, called her to report that a patient with prostate cancer who received morphine was barely breathing. Twaddle decided to visit the man herself.

"What is it that hurts?" she asks.

The man mumbles something about a machine.

Twaddle eventually understood: The patient is an octogenarian Russian immigrant who doesn't understand much English. "He had experienced the Holocaust, and now they're taking him down every day to a machine for radiation. So when they put him on the gurney, he says he's in pain."

She shakes her head. "You don't treat anxiety and fear with morphine. You treat anxiety and fear with education and support."

This is what hospice staff mean by holistic or palliative medicine: Their medical gaze sees beyond the disease itself. Though important, the hospice contribution to pain management represents only part of its strategy of care. Its support for palliative medicine may prove to be the movement's most important legacy.

> *The hospice contribution to pain management represents only part of its strategy of care. Its support for palliative medicine may prove to be the movement's most important legacy.*

Palliative care studies are now appearing at major universities, hospitals, and research centers. The United Hospital Fund in New York City has organized a 12-hospital project to test palliative care programs. D.C.'s George Washington University researchers have set up a Center to Improve Care of the Dying. The federal Assisted Suicide Funding Restriction Act, passed last year, authorizes HHS to fund research projects that emphasize palliative medicine to improve care for the terminally ill.

Oddly enough, until the doctor-assisted suicide debate, the hospice philosophy of care was not acknowledged by the medical establishment. The nation's top medical schools, the American Medical Association, the College of Physicians, the Institute of Medicine, and the National Academy of Science all mostly ignored the movement and its aims.

"They all acted as if hospice was a friendly aunt who would sit and hold the hand of a patient, but not anything serious adults needed to pay attention to," Byock says. "But now hospice is being recognized as a robust, medically competent, team-based approach to the person and family who are confronting life's end.". . . .

Living Until They Die

Even the goal of easing people's suffering, as central as it is to hospice care, is not an end in itself. The aim of comfort is part of a larger objective: to help the terminally ill live as fully as possible until they die. This is where hospice departs most pointedly both from traditional medicine and the advocates of assisted suicide.

Hospice, by shining a light on the emotional and spiritual aspects of suffering, is challenging the medical community to re-examine its priorities. The period at the end of life, simultaneously ignored and micromanaged by conventional approaches, can be filled with significance. To neglect it is to diminish ourselves. "Spiritual inattentiveness in the face of dying and death can lead to the sad spectacle of medical technology run amok," says Laurence O'Connell, the president of the Park Ridge Center, a medical ethics think tank in Chicago.

Those who have spent years tending to the dying say there is a mystery at life's end, one that seems to defy the rules of medicine. Walter Hunter, a medical director at the Hospice of Michigan, recalls a patient with end-stage kidney disease who entered hospice and quickly asked to be taken off of the hemodialysis (a kidney machine) needed to keep her alive. Conventional medical wisdom put her life expectancy at two to three weeks without the technology, but the woman said she was eager to die.

> *Hospice . . . is challenging the medical community to re-examine its priorities. The period at the end of life, simultaneously ignored and micromanaged by conventional approaches, can be filled with significance.*

Eight months later she was still alive. She asked Hunter, then her primary doctor, why she was still breathing. "I don't know," the doctor replied. "According to the textbooks, you should be dead."

Hospice staff had been busy in those months, keeping the patient comfortable, providing emotional and spiritual support. They later learned that just two days before the woman died, she had reconciled with one of her estranged children.

Sharon McCarthy has been a social worker at the Palliative CareCenter of the North Shore for 18 years. She has cared for thousands of dying patients, getting a ringside seat to the grief of countless families. For the vast majority, she says, hospice provides the window of opportunity to get their lives in order. One of the most common desires: forgiveness, both extended and received. "There's a lot of non-physical pain that goes on when these things aren't done." Says Mary Sheehan, director of clinical services and a 12-year veteran in hospice: "Ninety-nine percent of the time they have unfinished business."

Saving the Soul of Medicine

Hospice or hemlock: Though both end in death, each pursues its vision of a "good death" along radically different paths. At its deepest level, the hospice philosophy strikes a blow at the notion of the isolated individual. It insists that no one dies in a vacuum. Where one exists, hospice physicians, nurses, and social workers rush in to help fill it.

For many hospice staff and supporters, such work is motivated and informed by a deeply moral and religious outlook. "I do not work within a specific religious context," writes Byock in *Dying Well*, "but I find more than a little truth in the spiritual philosophies of Christianity, Buddhism, and Judaism." Karen Bell, the hospice director of the Catholic-run Providence Health System in Portland, Oregon, says her organization is propelled by religious values. "The foundational principle is that life has a meaning and value until the very end, regardless of a person's physical condition or mental state."

Faith communities have always been involved in caring for the desperately ill, founding hospitals, clinics, medical schools, and so on. Though not usually connected to religious institutions, nearly all hospice programs make spiritual counseling available; rabbis, chaplains, and ecumenical ministers make frequent home visits and regularly attend hospice team meetings.

For many religious physicians, tackling the issue of personal autonomy is a crucial step in end-of-life care. "This is the Christian answer to whose life it is: 'It is not your own; you were bought at a price,'" says Yale University Medical School's

Dr. Diane Komp, quoting the apostle Paul. "But if we are not in control of our lives, then we need companionship. We need the companionship of God and the companionship of those who reflect the image of God in this broken world."

Leon Kass, a physician and philosopher at the University of Chicago, says the religiously inspired moral vigor of hospice sets itself squarely against the movement for assisted death. "Hospice borrows its energy from a certain Judeo-Christian view of our obligations to suffering humanity," he says. "It is the idea that company and care, rather than attempts at cure, are abiding human obligations. These obligations are put to the severest test when the recipient of care is at his lowest and most unattractive."

We seem, as a culture, to be under such a test, and the outcome is not at all certain. Some call it a war for the soul of medicine. If so, hospice personnel could be to medical care what American GIs were to the Allied effort in Europe—the source of both its tactical and moral strength and, eventually, the foot soldiers for victory and reconstruction.

4

Advance Directives Help People Cope with Death

Harvard Women's Health Watch

Harvard Health Publications publishes information about health and wellness through all types of media.

Specifically documenting one's health care wishes in advance ensures that these wishes will be carried out in the event of a medical emergency that renders one unable to speak. Two kinds of advance directives—naming a health care proxy and preparing a detailed living will —are available. A health care proxy is someone selected ahead of time to speak on one's behalf regarding important medical decisions. A living will provides a written record specifying medical procedures that should or should not be used. Neither of these options is irreversible: An advance directive goes into effect only when one is incapacitated. Physicians who disagree with an advance directive and do not want to carry it out are legally obligated to locate another physician who will. Without advance directives, important medical decisions may be left up to strangers or to people who are unfamiliar with one's values or preferences.

Have you ever thought about what would happen if a serious illness or medical emergency left you unconscious? How will doctors know what treatments you want, or don't want? Who would communicate your wishes to them?

Unless you have a living will or health care proxy—documents known as *advance care directives*—important medical decisions may be left to a physician or others who are unaware of

Harvard Women's Health Watch, "Living Wills and Health Care Proxies," vol. 11, January 2004, pp. 6–7. Copyright © 2004 by the President and Fellows of Harvard College, www.health.harvard.edu. Reproduced by permission.

your values, beliefs, or preferences. Or a relative who doesn't know your wishes may make decisions for you when your best friend, who knows more about you, has no say legally.

We all hope our health will stay sound for the rest of our lives, and we do many things to protect it. However, life can throw a curve our way. That's why everyone over age 18 should have a living will or health care proxy.

What Do They Do?

The two types of advance care directives work in different ways. A *health care proxy* allows you to appoint someone as your health care agent—a person who will convey your wishes to medical personnel if you're unable to communicate. A *living will* lets you specify in writing what you want done in certain circumstances.

People sometimes worry that signing one of these documents means giving up control over their medical treatment. But that's not how they work. As long as you're able to make and communicate your decisions, your word supersedes anything you've written or said to others. An advance care directive goes into effect only when you're unconscious or too ill to make your wishes known. Once you recover enough to make and express your decisions, what you say takes precedence over any document.

Advance care directives are not difficult to understand, and you don't need a lawyer's help. Some experts suggest that you either make a living will *or* assign a health care proxy. If you choose to have both, naming a health care agent should be your first priority. This ensures that someone can act on your behalf in situations not covered in a living will.

The Health Care Proxy

In this document, you name a person to make health care choices for you if you can't make the decisions yourself. If you don't have a health care proxy, that job will likely fall to your relatives. For many people, this isn't a problem. But unless you feel close to your legal next of kin, you may not want decisions about your health care in his or her hands. Also, if two or more relatives are at your bedside, your clinicians may feel they must seek a consensus before proceeding. This can cause conflict and delay treatment.

It's best not to appoint more than one agent (and in many states it's illegal to do so), because all of them would need to agree on every decision. But do appoint an alternate agent in the event your first agent is unavailable when needed. You can also instruct your agent to consult others.

Your health care agent is legally obligated to make decisions that she or he thinks you would make. That's why it's important to be as specific as possible with your agent about medical treatments you may or may not want, your religious or spiritual beliefs, and your preferences in situations that might arise. You can't anticipate everything, so make sure you feel absolutely comfortable allowing the person you choose to decide about matters you haven't specifically discussed.

What's in a Living Will?

If you don't know anyone who would make a good health care agent for you, don't choose one. Filling out a state-specific living will is better than appointing someone who might not carry out your wishes. A living will provides a written record that can guide your doctors and loved ones in caring for you. In many instances, it's used to determine how aggressive your medical treatment will be.

> **As long as you're able to make and communicate your decisions, your word supersedes anything you've written or said to others.**

Living wills generally ask about the following medical procedures:

Artificial nutrition and hydration (tube feeding): This procedure involves placing a tube in a vein, the stomach, or the upper intestine when a person is unable to eat and drink. People who reject tube feeding often do so because of the discomfort or because tube feeding may lead to other invasive procedures.

Cardiopulmonary resuscitation (CPR): CPR can be used in an attempt to save the life of a person who has gone into cardiac arrest. Toward the end of life, the chance of success is very low, and CPR can cause injury. Some people with terminal illnesses who have been resuscitated this way say they wish they hadn't been.

Defibrillation: An electric shock may restart the heart when it fails. The shock causes the body to jerk, although the person is usually unconscious and doesn't feel it. Some people who are sick or dying decide to forgo defibrillation because they feel it's "too much."

> **❝** *Unless you feel close to your legal next of kin, you may not want decisions about your health care in his or her hands.* **❞**

Mechanical ventilation: A ventilator or respirator (sometimes called a "breathing machine") forces air into the lungs when a patient can't breathe adequately on her own. A tube attached to the machine is inserted into the nose, mouth, or throat and passed into the trachea (windpipe). Because of the extreme discomfort, a person on a ventilator requires high doses of sedatives and thus is not fully conscious. People decline this procedure for many reasons. They may not want their families to see them in an incoherent state, hooked up to a machine. Many simply don't want to spend what may be their last days lying in a hospital bed on life support.

Pressors: These are medications, delivered through an intravenous tube, that raise blood pressure. Pressors are generally used only for the sickest patients. Some people feel that if their condition is that severe, they'd prefer not to have any intervention.

Sharing Your Health Care Preferences

After your agent, your doctor is the most important person to talk to about your living will or health care proxy. She or he can also provide you with information about how various treatments might affect you. Schedule an appointment specifically for this purpose, or arrange for extra time at your next visit.

A doctor who disagrees with your wishes doesn't have to carry them out, but is obligated to find another clinician who will. To avoid or address this complication, make sure your doctor is aware of the contents of your advance care directive and agrees to find a clinician to comply with any requests that she or he finds problematic.

Be sure your physician knows your preferences about pain management. Also, let him or her know how much you want to know—and how much you want shared with your family—about your condition, should you become very ill.

It's important to define any terms in your health care proxy or living will that could be open to interpretation, such as "life-threatening," "short period of time," "severe disease," "end-stage condition," and, especially, "quality of life." In a study reported in the November 1, 2003, *British Medical Journal*, a group of doctors given a hypothetical living will and patient story came to very different conclusions about what should be done. Clarifying terms, the authors suggest, can help everyone involved better understand and act on patients' wishes.

Once you've completed your advance care directive, keep the original and ask your doctor to keep a copy in your medical file along with his or her notes about the conversations you've had. If you have a health care agent, be sure his or her contact information is in the file and kept current.

5

Advance Directives Do Not Help People Cope with Death

Nancy Valko

Nancy Valko, a longtime advocate of patients with disabili-ties, writes the regular "Bioethics Watch" column for
Voices. *A registered nurse since 1969, she is president of Missouri Nurses for Life. She is also a spokeswoman for the National Association of Pro-life Nurses, a board member of Missouri Right to Life, and past cochair of the Saint Louis Archdiocesan Pro-Life Committee.*

A living will provides a written record specifying what medical procedures a person wants should he or she be-come incapacitated. Though living wills purport to ease the dying process, they can create more problems than they solve. For one thing, a patient's inability to partic-ipate in the medical decision-making process may be temporary, but the living will can result in the person's death before he or she regains consciousness. Also, physicians who worry about lawsuits may withhold treatment for those who have a living will. Another problem is that terminology included in many living wills is open to various interpretations, leaving open the possibility that a patient's wishes will not be met. No living will is risk free. A better alternative is to select a friend or relative to speak on one's behalf.

Who can forget the infamous "butterfly ballot"? In [the 2000] presidential election, there were allegations that the butterfly ballot—one with candidates on both sides of the ballot and arrows pointing to the appropriate hole to be punched—confused elderly Florida voters into voting for the wrong candidate and thus gave Governor [George W.] Bush the election.

But in terms of potential confusion—for young and old alike—the butterfly ballot has nothing on the "living will". While confusion about ballots is terrible, confusion about matters like the "living will" can be lethal.

For example, earlier this year [2001], I received a call from a woman concerned about her 100-year-old mother, who was living in a nursing home. "Joyce" worried that her mother, "Alice", wasn't receiving adequate medical care and food. She cited an instance where she wanted her mother to be taken to the hospital for treatment of pneumonia and dehydration.

> The 'living will' was originally invented in 1967 by two groups, the Euthanasia Society of America and Euthanasia Education Council, and was touted as a first step in gaining public acceptance of euthanasia.

The problem was that the elderly woman had signed a "living will" eight years before, and listed her son rather than her daughter as the person to make medical decisions. And, according to the daughter who called me, the son was reluctant to authorize any more treatment for his mother because he felt it was time for her to die. Alice, the mom, was now frail and needed help with eating and bathing but was conscious, though usually confused. In cases like this, nursing homes and other institutions rely on the "living will" and other advance directives as the ultimate legal arbiter. The daughter now had no say in her mother's treatment and was even threatened with being barred from seeing her.

Is this what Alice envisioned when she signed her "living will" and, in effect, "voted" for non-treatment?

History of the "Living Will"

Very few people signing "living wills" and other advance directives have any idea of how such documents became a universal aspect of health care today.

In the early 1970s when I was a young nurse, we had never heard of the "living will". When a patient was confused or comatose and appeared to be dying, we discussed such possibilities as "do not resuscitate" (DNR) orders with families. Often, aggressive or useless treatments were discouraged because such measures were considered futile or excessively burdensome in that situation. But one thing we didn't do was offer to withhold or withdraw treatments like antibiotics or feedings to cause or hasten the patient's death.

> **❝** Horror stories about doctors overtreating dying patients . . . led people to believe that the 'living will' was a necessity. **❞**

This all began to change with the advent of the "living will" and the increasing acceptance of the newly discovered "right to die".

Actually, the "living will" was originally invented in 1967 by two groups, the Euthanasia Society of America and Euthanasia Education Council, and was touted as a first step in gaining public acceptance of euthanasia. These groups had been struggling for years to get "mercy-killing" bills (which would allow doctors to give disabled or dying patients lethal overdoses) passed in various state legislatures. The "living will" opened up the new strategy of an incremental approach.

Along with the "living will", these groups also made strategic name changes: The Euthanasia Society of America changed into the Society for the Right to Die and the Euthanasia Education Council became Concern for Dying. In the 1990s, the groups formally merged and are now known simply as Choice in Dying.

The First "Living Wills"

The first "living wills" were simple declarations such as "If I should have a terminal illness and I am unable to make medical decisions, I direct my attending physician to withhold or withdraw medical treatment that prolongs the dying process and is not necessary to my comfort or to alleviate my pain". Horror

stories about doctors overtreating dying patients—which sometimes happens—led people to believe that the "living will" was
a necessity. California became the first state to legalize the "living will" in 1976, as the California Natural Death Act. Eventually all other states followed suit. But there were some concerns.

> *The 'right to die' position [morphed] from one
> where the issue was allowing dying people a
> natural death to one where choice and legalities
> were the primary issues, whatever the patient's
> condition.*

In Missouri, pro-life advocates noted the beginning of court
cases involving the removal of feeding tubes from non-dying,
brain-injured people now called "vegetative" and they feared
the "living will" would allow such passive euthanasia. "Right to
die" advocates in Missouri disavowed this and, to ensure passage of the pending "living will" bill, a provision was added that
food and water were among the kinds of care and treatment
that could not be withdrawn. That provision was short-lived.

Euthanasia advocates soon bemoaned the "limitations" of
the "living will" and proposed a new document called the
"durable powers of attorney for health care" (DPA). This new
kind of "living will" allowed another person, usually a relative
or friend, to be named to make all health care decisions when-
ever a person was mentally incapacitated. It also usually added
the newly invented term "permanent vegetative state" and a
checklist of the types of treatment to be automatically refused.

The Need for "Safeguards"

In response, states like Missouri and New York passed "safeguards" to ensure that feeding tubes could not be removed
without "clear and convincing" evidence that the person
would have wanted feedings removed if in a "vegetative" state.
This was about more than just the "vegetative" state. It allowed
the "right to die" position to morph from one where the issue
was allowing dying people a natural death to one where choice
and legalities were the primary issues, whatever the patient's
condition.

This set the stage for the Nancy Cruzan[1] feeding tube case in Missouri, which gave the biggest boost yet to the "right to die" agenda.

Nancy's parents, with the help of "right to die" advocates, petitioned a local judge for permission to withdraw Nancy's feeding tube despite the lack of "clear and convincing" evidence that this is what she would have wanted. This case of a woman said to be in a "vegetative" state for seven years gained national notoriety, and eventually reached the US Supreme Court, which upheld Missouri's "clear and convincing" standard.

But public sympathy for Nancy's parents was enormous and the case went back to the local judge who first ruled that the feeding tube could be removed. Three of Nancy's former friends then came forward to testify that, about ten years previously, Nancy had seemed to agree with statements about not wanting to live in an incapacitated state. The judge determined that these statements met the "clear and convincing" standard and Nancy died twelve long days after her feedings were stopped.

The 1991 Patient Self-Determination Act

In reaction to the Cruzan decision, the US Congress enabled the Patient Self-Determination Act (PSDA) to be enacted in 1991. Proposed by Missouri Senator John Danforth and New York Senator Daniel Patrick Moynihan, the PSDA mandated that all patients be offered information and documents on their right to refuse treatment and thus prevent another Cruzan case. Hospitals were threatened with loss of federal funding if they did not comply.

> *'Living wills' are often interpreted by doctors and nurses as meaning the patient would rather die than live with a significant disability.*

Despite this, "right to die" advocates were disappointed that relatively few prospective patients actually sign a "living will" or other advance directives. But they were heartened by the media

---

1. A 1983 auto accident left Cruzan permanently unconscious and without any higher brain function.

and public acceptance of the "right to die", which made withdrawal of treatment decisions common, whether or not a "living will" was signed. "Right to die" advocates then set their sights on "physician-assisted suicide", using the Nancy Cruzan case to make their case that, since death was the goal of withdrawing feedings from the "vegetative", a constitutional "right to die" should allow lethal overdoses for conscious, terminally ill persons. The US Supreme Court didn't buy this argument, but opened the door for states to "experiment". Oregon passed the first assisted suicide law in 1994 (in effect in 1997).

> *Documents can cause more problems and confusion than they claim to 'solve'.*

Now, the "right to die" mentality has so thoroughly permeated health care that even Catholic medical ethics committees discuss "futility guidelines", designed to overrule families or patients who want care continued when a patient is deemed to have a poor quality of life. Some prominent ethicists now recommend rationing health care and denying many routine medical treatments to patients over a certain age. "Living wills" are often interpreted by doctors and nurses as meaning the patient would rather die than live with a significant disability. Families are encouraged to make non-treatment decisions as soon as possible after illnesses such as strokes and asked "would your mom really want to live like this?" Coupled with the current cost-containment mania in health care, the "right to die" is fast becoming the "duty to die".

Alice's "Living Will"

As a nurse, I have seen all types of "living wills" over the years. Some are very long and full of legalese. Some are short and vague. One-hundred-year-old Alice's "living will" is typical of many offered today—even in Catholic health care facilities—and contains both a "living will" and a kind of DPA. Alice's "living will", when examined, shows how such documents can cause more problems and confusion than they claim to "solve".

The first page contains the usual terminology about "an incurable injury, disease or illness certified to be a terminal condition . . . where the application of life-sustaining procedures would serve only to artificially prolong the dying process and I am unable to participate in decisions regarding my medical treatment, I direct that such procedures be withheld or withdrawn".

Unfortunately, while Alice may have envisioned a coma-like state and a condition such as cancer, the reality is that such conditions as a severe stroke or Alzheimer's are often considered terminal conditions even though the person can live for a long time afterwards. And the "inability to participate in making decisions" can be temporary or permanent and even include conscious states such as simple confusion.

On the second page of Alice's document, as usual, there is the instruction that "if there is a statement below with which you do not agree, draw a line through it and add your initials." (Try adding this instruction to a voting ballot in Florida and hear the howls of "confusing" and "unfair".)

> **//** Unlike consent forms, 'living wills' and other advance directives are not used to inform people about the risks and benefits before treatment in a particular situation. **//**

Alice's document goes on to say that it is "the final expression of my legal right to refuse medical or surgical treatment and accept the consequences of such refusal". This exempts the doctor from any legal risk regarding withholding or withdrawing treatment but, ironically, has led to lawsuits where a doctor does provide treatment and the patient survives but is debilitated. Many health care professionals now feel that the safest course when a patient has a "living will" is "if in doubt, do not treat".

Unintended Consequences

The second page of Alice's document expands the terminal condition to "a condition, disease or injury without hope of significant recovery, or extreme mental deterioration or other (fill in the blank)". The document goes on: "Life-sustaining procedures I choose to have withheld or withdrawn include: surgery, heart-lung resuscitation (CPR), antibiotics, mechanical ventilator (respirator), tube feeding (food and water delivered through a tube in the vein, nose or stomach), and other (fill in the blank)" and "a meaningful quality of life means to me that: (fill in the blank)".

The document also conveniently provides permission for organ donation.

Alice, like most people signing such a document, did not cross off anything or fill in the blanks. This left Alice vulnerable to such possibilities as the denial of simple antibiotics if she contracted pneumonia or the withholding of surgery if she fractured her hip. And terms like "significant recovery", "extreme mental deterioration" and "meaningful life" have no real medical meaning and are thus open to various interpretations by doctors or families.

Unlike consent forms, "living wills" and other advance directives are not used to inform people about the risks and benefits before treatment in a particular situation. Instead, they are used to cover refusal of treatment in an unknown future situation, which can lead to unintended consequences.

> *While it has always been true that futile or excessively burdensome treatment or care can be morally refused, the Church has long condemned causing or hastening death, whether by omission or commission.*

For example, in 1988 my own mother was fully conscious but in a moderate stage of Alzheimer's disease when a growth was discovered in her throat. Surgery was performed and the doctor informed us that the growth was an incurable cancer wrapped around her windpipe. During surgery, he performed a tracheostomy, a hole in her throat. My family was aghast at this and when the doctor started talking about chemotherapy and radiation, they drove him from the room. They assumed the doctor was trying to prolong Mom's dying. And, indeed, if my Mom had signed a "living will" like Alice's, she would have felt comfortable checking off surgery, chemotherapy and radiation as death-prolonging treatment to be refused.

What my family didn't know was that the tracheostomy was performed to prevent future suffocation as the tumor grew.

The chemo and radiation were proposed as palliative therapy, hopefully to prevent or minimize the pain as the cancer grew in that sensitive area.

After the dust settled, I explained all this to my father who then authorized the treatments. Mom tolerated them well and, although no guarantees were made, she didn't even need a Tylenol for pain at the end. Three months after the surgery she died as predicted and just the way she wanted—peacefully in her sleep. I shudder to think what might have happened if Mom had a "living will" and no one to explain options.

Resisting the New "Death Ethics"

Even Catholic hospitals and nursing homes now offer the kind of "living will" Alice had and, sadly, most people falsely assume that such directives are automatically compatible with Church teaching.

While it has always been true that futile or excessively burdensome treatment or care can morally be refused, the Church has long condemned causing or hastening death, whether by omission or commission.

In 1998, Pope John [Paul] II said that "a great teaching effort is needed to clarify the substantive moral difference between discontinuing medical procedures that may be burdensome, dangerous, or disproportionate to the expected outcome [what the Catechism of the Catholic Church calls "the refusal of 'over-zealous' treatment"] and taking away the ordinary means of preserving life, such as feeding, hydration, and normal medical care". Unfortunately, some Catholic ethicists have influenced Catholic health care facilities to follow the secular, "right to die" ethic instead.

> *It is also crucial that you choose a doctor without a 'right to die' bias, preferably one with a good understanding of traditional ethical principles.*

Groups like National Right to Life, American Life League and the International Anti-Euthanasia Task Force have developed more protective documents like the "Will to Live" and

"Loving Will", to address many of the problems in the standard "living will" or other advance directives. These documents can be useful, especially when family members disagree about ethical options, but they are not usually available at hospitals and nursing homes. The documents can be obtained by contacting the organizations themselves or sometimes through pro-life organizations. . . .

However, no "living will" is risk-free and even refusing to sign a "living will" is no guarantee that the "right to die" will not be exercised for you despite your wishes.

The best defense now is to have a loving relative or friend who is informed about ethical options and who can legally speak for you if you cannot because of illness or injury. It is also crucial that you choose a doctor without a "right to die" bias, preferably one with a good understanding of traditional ethical principles.

As a former hospice nurse and current ICU [intensive care unit] nurse, I can attest that there is a very real difference between allowing natural death and hastening or causing a person's death.

The Culture of Death spawned the "living will" and it has been very successful in seducing society to increasingly ignore this difference, even to the point of accepting assisted suicide. We continue down this slippery slope at our own peril.

6

Belief in God Can Ease the Dying Process

Myles N. Sheehan

Myles N. Sheehan is senior associate dean and associate professor of internal medicine at Loyola University. His special interests include aging and dementia. A practicing Jesuit priest, Sheehan also helped to develop the geriatrics curriculum at Harvard Medical School.

Though dying is neither easy nor pleasant, learning how to prepare for one's death so that one can die well is essential. First, dying well means that one should put medical care in proper perspective. A doctor should be attentive to one's wishes and should not attempt to interfere with the dying process when death is clearly at hand. Death should be seen not only as an end of earthly life but as the beginning of life spent with God. Second, dying well means that one should feel no guilt about refusing life-sustaining care when such care only prolongs suffering and death. Third, dying well requires that one live well before death comes, especially when it comes to one's faith. This means growing in intimacy with God and living a good life.

In the last few years, I have become increasingly involved with death.

This involvement has come from three sources: my clinical practice as a physician specializing in geriatrics, my work as a Jesuit priest at an academic medical center and my own attempts as an educator to improve the care of the dying. I spend much of my time caring for dying persons, teaching medical students and physicians about end-of-life care and working with priests, parish leaders and others to mine the resources of our Catholic faith's traditions about the end of life.

More than once, I have wondered what my own dying will be like and whether or not I will die well. Such musings usually revolve around what "dying well" means and thinking about the presence of God as I am called from this life. The particular circumstances of my life, as a Jesuit priest who will die without wife and children, make my own planning a bit idiosyncratic and not readily accessible to the vast bulk of the population who are not vowed religious. But let me share a bit of advice about what I mean and how I think about dying well.

It Is OK to Be Afraid

Dying well does not mean dying stoically. I have no doubt I will be afraid. The thought of leaving the warm sun over Cape Cod Bay, the sound of a trout stream in Montana and the embrace and comfort of my friends and their children is not something that I am thrilled about. But in my life I have come to know my God as someone who is fairly used to my fears and anxieties. And I sense that the Lord deals with me a bit like a father who is trying to pull a toddler away from things that may transiently amuse but ultimately will not satisfy. Death will be the definitive tug into the arms of God.

> *Dying is not easy. There will always be existential distress and suffering for anyone conscious of decline and the loss of the good things of life.*

Dying has its own trajectory, sometimes short and steep, sometimes with recurring crises and transient improvement. What our death will be like depends largely on what we are dying from. Obviously, sudden death, whether from accident or a massive heart attack or stroke, does not have much of a trajectory. One is more or less fine, and then one is dead. It may be that there is an in-between phase, in which medical resources have been able to avert death but leave the person to die in a few days or weeks. Sometimes it may be that the previously well are saved from a catastrophe only to become chronically ill and follow a long downhill course.

Some illnesses, like cancer, may have a long period when the person is quite stable, doing well, active and able to function normally. Then, if the malignancy cannot be cured, there will come a period of decline, usually over a few months, where the individual will have diminishing functional abilities and require more medical intervention for symptom relief before ultimately succumbing.

> **Regrettably, many good people are in favor of assisted suicide because they have witnessed deaths that are bad, filled with pain and marred by needless suffering.**

Other illnesses, like advanced congestive heart failure, have more of a roller-coaster path to death. There are sudden crises when the lungs fill with fluid; there is a hospitalization, things get better, and then there are long periods of relative stability. If the underlying heart failure progresses, despite the use of added medications and the variety of tinkering available to care for this illness, the crises come more frequently and the in-between times are less good, with worsening shortness of breath, fatigue, decreased appetite and malaise.

A good death, regardless of the circumstances, means putting medical care in proper perspective and not allowing it to dominate. That is why thinking about the trajectory of illness is important. In sudden catastrophes, the role of the doctor and the health care team is to attempt to save lives. But when the outcome is less clear or the condition incurable, medicine needs to focus on palliation.

Free from Pain

The word palliate comes from the Latin pallium, meaning a shelter or cloak. Palliative care seeks to shelter the individual from the distress of illness, relieve symptoms and maintain function and comfort. Palliative care needs to be part of the care of all serious illness, regardless of how likely a cure may be. Too often, however, physicians and others do not think of conditions other than cancer as appropriate for palliation. Also, too often, we neglect to build palliation into the care plan for persons with cancer even when there are reasonable hopes for a cure, creating unnecessary suffering even if the ultimate outcome is a happy one. We are used to recognizing that individuals with advanced cancer will die and that we can shift our therapy and planning to focus on comfort and quality. But with other illnesses, like the advanced congestive heart failure described above, the pattern of sudden crises resolved by medical technology interspersed with periods of slow decline makes us neglect the need to face the fact that death is the inevitable outcome. As a consequence, a lot of effort goes into acute rescues rather than planning for decline and working hard on symptomatic relief.

Frightened by the propaganda of the death-seeking advocates of assisted suicide and euthanasia, many feel that dying is an inherently awful process. Dying is not easy. There will always be existential distress and suffering for anyone conscious of decline and the loss of the good things of life. I know I will be very sad over the end of listening to Mozart, the loss of the hugs of the children in my life and the sheer sweetness of so much of life. But I also know there is no reason for me to be in severe pain, uncomfortable from shortness of breath or desperate for relief from nausea and vomiting. Regrettably, many good people are in favor of assisted suicide because they have witnessed deaths that are bad, filled with pain and marred by needless suffering. These have occurred because physicians, hospitals and Americans have on the whole not made expert care of the dying a priority.

> *Putting medical care into its proper perspective means that patients and their families do not always grasp for more and put misplaced hope in doctors and treatments when dying is clearly at hand.*

This is now changing. Pain can be relieved without rendering a person unconscious. It takes some trial and error, and there will be times when pain medication needs to be readjusted or switched. Side effects of medication, like constipation, have to be anticipated and treated. Shortness of breath can be relieved by a variety of efforts, depending on the cause. And nausea and vomiting, although frequently difficult symptoms, can be effectively treated by the aggressive use of medication and other palliative therapies.

Planning for Death

Some may find it inherently morbid to think about things like the trajectory of dying and the kind of symptoms that can make death hard. I think it is essential if one wants to die well. Dying well takes some planning and choices. It is not that we can control and stage manage every aspect of the dying process. Losing control is part of what it means to die. But we can make sure that our goals are respected as we face the end of our lives. . . .

> *Dying well means living well with God. Preparation for death should be an everyday affair for the Christian.*

First, medical care needs to be put in proper perspective. No one gets out of this life alive. Doctors can cure us for a while, they can relieve our suffering as we are dying, and they can do a good job of obstructing death when we are clearly dying, if we are so dumb as to let them. A good death for me will require a good doctor. This means that the doctor will be attentive to my wishes, vigilant about symptom control and pain relief; that he or she will be a prudent advisor in the face of sadness and fear, and sensitive to the dynamic that life is never to be taken deliberately but need not be prolonged when the burdens of therapy outweigh the benefits to the patient. But it is also important that medical care not be the focus of dying. The doctor and the other members of the care team are not the stars of the show when we come to the last act. They have important supporting roles.

The key players, however, are the person who is dying, those who love him and God. A good doctor will be clear about the limitations of her art. One sometimes hears physicians say to a person: "I am sorry, but there is nothing more that can be done." A better response is that of the physician who is wise enough to state: "I have no magic treatment, no new drug, no surgery that is likely to change the course of your disease. But I promise to be with you, to relieve your symptoms and never to abandon you to the experience of your illness." Putting medical care into its proper perspective means that patients and their families do not always grasp for more and put misplaced hope in doctors and treatments when dying is clearly at hand. In the light of eternal life, and our hope in the resurrection, relentless efforts to prolong the dying process of someone with an incurable illness can seem somewhere between silly and blasphemous.

Second, dying well for people of faith who are Catholic means sensitivity to the moral tradition of the church. This requires finding the mean between those who reject any sort of life-sustaining care and those who think that being Catholic requires that every possible tube and treatment must be thrust upon a person before one can die. The former attitude comes close to euthanasia in its lack of appreciation of the goodness of life and the need to value the gift that God has given us. The second attitude replaces faith in God with vitalism; it suggests that every heartbeat is sacred rather than realizing that life's absolute value is found in union with God.

Practically speaking, when one is facing a terminal illness the wisdom of the church is that one is not obliged to pursue treatments that are painful, difficult to bear or simply prolong dying. A person who has cancer or advanced emphysema, or is facing the last stages of decline from heart failure should not feel that there is any moral problem in refusing to be resuscitated or declining the aggressive high technology care offered in the intensive care unit.

Third, and most important, dying well means living well with God. Preparation for death should be an everyday affair for the Christian, not in the sense that one is continually revising advance directives or wondering about potential moral conflicts, but in the daily effort to grow in intimacy with the Lord and to live one's life well. Although planning for death with advance directives, good medical care and moral sensitivity are important, the essential part of dying well is living in Christ.

7

Recognizing a Duty to Die Can Help People Die with Dignity

John Hardwig

John Hardwig teaches medical ethics and social political philosophy at East Tennessee State University. He is also the author of Is There a Duty to Die? *and Other Essays in Bioethics.*

A concern among many who are opposed to physician-assisted suicide is that if it were to become legal, some people might feel they have a duty to die in order to avoid becoming a burden either to loved ones or to society. Thus the notion of having a duty to die is associated with negative feelings. However, medical advances are prolonging people's lives to the extent that most individuals become demented or otherwise incapacitated as age advances. Because people are interconnected, such debilitation places a burden on others to take care of the terminally ill—often causing emotional and economic hardship. It is incumbent upon all individuals to determine whether that hardship is worth extending their lives for a few months or whether there may, in fact, be a duty to die.

When [former Colorado governor] Richard Lamm made the statement [in a 1984 address] that old people have a duty to die, it was generally shouted down or ridiculed. The whole idea is just too preposterous to entertain. Or too threatening. In fact, a fairly common argument against legalizing physician-

John Hardwig, "Is There a Duty to Die?" *Hastings Center Report*, 1997, pp. 34–42. Copyright © 1997 by *Hastings Center Report*. Reproduced by permission of the publisher and the author.

assisted suicide is that if it were legal, some people might somehow get the idea that they have a duty to die. These people could only be the victims of twisted moral reasoning or vicious social pressure. It goes without saying that there is no duty to die.

But for me the question is real and very important. I feel strongly that I may very well some day have a duty to die. I do not believe that I am idiosyncratic, morbid, mentally ill, or morally perverse in thinking this. I think many of us will eventually face precisely this duty. But I am first of all concerned with my own duty. I write partly to clarify my own convictions and to prepare myself. Ending my life might be a very difficult thing for me to do.

> *The costs—and these are not merely monetary—of prolonging our lives when we are no longer able to care for ourselves are often staggering.*

This notion of a duty to die raises all sorts of interesting theoretical and metaethical questions. I intend to try to avoid most of them because I hope my argument will be persuasive to those holding a wide variety of ethical views. Also, although the claim that there is a duty to die would ultimately require theoretical underpinning, the discussion needs to begin on the normative level.

I will use "duty," "obligation," and "responsibility" interchangeably, in a pretheoretical or preanalytic sense, as is appropriate to my attempt to steer clear of theoretical commitments.

Circumstances and a Duty to Die

Do many of us really believe that no one ever has a duty to die? I suspect not. I think most of us probably believe that there is such a duty, but it is very uncommon. Consider Captain Oates, a member of Admiral Scott's expedition to the South Pole. Oates became too ill to continue. If the rest of the team stayed with him, they would all perish. After this had become clear, Oates left his tent one night, walked out into a raging blizzard, and was never seen again. That may have been a heroic thing.

This is a very unusual circumstance—a "lifeboat case"—and

lifeboat cases make for bad ethics. But I expect that most of us would also agree that there have been cultures in which what we would call a duty to die has been fairly common. These are relatively poor, technologically simple, and especially nomadic cultures. In such societies, everyone knows that if you manage to live long enough, you will eventually become old and debilitated. Then you will need to take steps to end your life. The old people in these societies regularly did precisely that. Their cultures prepared and supported them in doing so.

Those cultures could be dismissed as irrelevant to contemporary bioethics; their circumstances are so different from ours. But if that is our response, it is instructive. It suggests that we assume a duty to die is irrelevant to us because of our wealth and technological sophistication have purchased exemption for us . . . except under very unusual circumstances like Captain Oates'.

But have wealth and technology really exempted us? Or are they, on the contrary, about to make a duty to die common again? We like to think of modern medicine as all triumph with no dark side at all. Our medicine saves many lives and enables most of us to live longer. That is wonderful, indeed. We are all glad to have access to this medicine. But our medicine also delivers most of us over to chronic illnesses and it enables many of us to survive longer than we can take care of ourselves, longer than we know what to do with ourselves, longer than we even are ourselves.

> *We are not a race of hermits. Illness and death do not come only to those who are all alone.*

The costs—and these are not merely monetary—of prolonging our lives when we are no longer able to care for ourselves are often staggering. If further medical advances wipe out many of today's "killer diseases"—cancers, heart attacks, strokes, ALS, AIDS, and the rest—then one day most of us will survive long enough to become demented or debilitated. These developments could generate a fairly widespread duty to die. A fairly common duty to die might turn out to be only the dark side of our life-prolonging medicine and the uses we choose to make of it.

Let me be clear. I certainly believe that there is a duty to refuse life-prolonging medical treatment and also a duty to complete advance directives refusing life-prolonging treatment. But a duty to die can go well beyond that. There can be a duty to die before one's illnesses would cause death, even if treated only with palliative measures. In fact, there may be a fairly common responsibility to end one's life in the absence of any terminal illness at all. Finally, there can be a duty to die when one would prefer to live. Granted, many of the conditions that can generate a duty to die also seriously undermine the quality of life. Some prefer not to live under such conditions. But even those who want to live can face a duty to die. These will clearly be the most controversial and troubling cases; I will, accordingly, focus my reflections on them.

The Individualistic Fantasy

Because a duty to die seems such a real possibility to me, I wonder why contemporary bioethics has dismissed it without serious consideration. I believe that most bioethics still shares in one of our deeply embedded American dreams: the individualistic fantasy. This fantasy leads us to imagine that lives are separate and unconnected, or that they could be so if we chose. If lives were unconnected, things that happened in my life would not or need not affect others. And if others were not (much) affected by my life, I would have no duty to consider the impact of my decisions on others. I would then be morally free to live my life however I please, choosing whatever life and death I prefer for myself. The way I live would be nobody's business but my own. I certainly would have no duty to die if I preferred to live.

> *The burdens of providing care or even just supervision twenty-four hours a day, seven days a week are often overwhelming.*

Within a health care context, the individualistic fantasy leads us to assume that the patient is the only one affected by decisions about her medical treatment. If only the patient were affected, the relevant questions when making treatment decisions would be precisely those we ask: What will benefit the patient? Who can best decide that? The pivotal issue would always be simply whether the patient herself wants to live like this and whether she herself would be better off dead. "Whose life is it, anyway?" we ask rhetorically.

> *It is out of these responsibilities that a duty to die can develop.*

But this is morally obtuse. We are not a race of hermits. Illness and death do not come only to those who are all alone. Nor is it much better to think in terms of the bald dichotomy between "the interests of the patient" and "the interests of society" (or a third-party payer), as if we were isolated individuals connected only to "society" in the abstract or to the other, faceless members of our health maintenance organization.

Most of us are affiliated with particular others and most deeply, with family and loved ones. Families and loved ones are bound together by ties of care and affection, by legal relations and obligations, by inhabiting shared spaces and living units, by interlocking finances and economic prospects, by common projects and also commitments to support the different life projects of other family members, by shared histories, by ties of loyalty. This life together of family and loved ones is what defines and sustains us; it is what gives meaning to most of our lives. We would not have it any other way. We would not want to be all alone, especially when we are seriously ill, as we age, and when we are dying.

A Burden to My Loved Ones

But many older people report that their one remaining goal in life is not to be a burden to their loved ones. Young people feel this, too: when I ask my undergraduate students to think about whether their death could come too late, one of their very first responses always is, "Yes, when I become a burden to my family or loved ones." Tragically, there are situations in which my loved ones would be much better off—all things considered, the loss of a loved one notwithstanding—if I were dead.

The lives of our loved ones can be seriously compromised by caring for us. The burdens of providing care or even just supervision twenty-four hours a day, seven days a week are often overwhelming. When this kind of caregiving goes on for years, it leaves the caregiver exhausted, with no time for herself or life of her own. Ultimately, even her health is often destroyed. But it can also be emotionally devastating simply to live with a spouse who is increasingly distant, uncommunicative, unresponsive, foreign, and unreachable. Other family members' needs often go unmet as the caring capacity of the family is exceeded. Social life and friendships evaporate, as there is no opportunity to go out to see friends and the home is no longer a place suitable for having friends in.

We must also acknowledge that the lives of our loved ones can be devastated just by having to pay for health care for us. One part of the recent SUPPORT study documented the financial aspects of caring for a dying member of a family. Only those who had illnesses severe enough to give them less than a 50% chance to live six more months were included in this study. When these patients survived their initial hospitalization and were discharged, about 1/3 required considerable caregiving from their families, in 20% of cases a family member had to quit work or make some other major lifestyle change, almost 1/3 of these families lost all of their savings, and just under 30% lost a major source of income.

> *There is deep irony in the fact that the very successes of our life-prolonging medicine help to create a widespread duty to die.*

If talking about money sounds venal or trivial, remember that much more than money is normally at stake here. When someone has to quit work, she may well lose her career. Savings decimated late in life cannot be recouped in the few remaining years of employability, so the loss compromises the quality of the rest of the caregiver's life. For a young person, the chance to go to college may be lost to the attempt to pay debts due to an illness in the family, and this decisively shapes an entire life.

A serious illness in a family is a misfortune. It is usually nobody's fault; no one is responsible for it. But we face choices about how we will respond to this misfortune. That's where the responsibility comes in and fault can arise. Those of us with families and loved ones always have a duty not to make selfish or self-centered decisions about our lives. We have a responsibility to try to protect the lives of loved ones from serious threats or greatly impoverished quality, certainly an obligation not to make choices that will jeopardize or seriously compromise their futures. Often, it would be wrong to do just what we want or just what is best for ourselves; we should choose in light of what is best for all concerned. That is our duty in sickness as well as in health. It is out of these responsibilities that a duty to die can develop.

> **We [cannot] conquer death by postponing it ever longer. We can conquer death only by finding meaning in it.**

I am not advocating a crass, quasi-economic conception of burdens and benefits, nor a shallow, hedonistic view of life. Given a suitably rich understanding of benefits, family members sometimes do benefit from suffering through the long illness of a loved one. Caring for the sick or aged can foster growth, even as it makes daily life immeasurably harder and the prospects for the future much bleaker. Chronic illness or a drawn-out death can also pull a family together, making the care for each other stronger and more evident. If my loved ones are truly benefiting from coping with my illness or debility, I have no duty to die based on burdens to them.

But it would be irresponsible to blithely assume that this always happens, that it will happen in my family, or that it will be the fault of my family if they can not manage to turn my illness into a positive experience. Perhaps the opposite is more common: a hospital chaplain once told me that he could not think of a single case in which a family was strengthened or brought together by what happened at the hospital.

Our families and loved ones also have obligations, of course—they have the responsibility to stand by us and to support us through debilitating illness and death. They must be prepared to make significant sacrifices to respond to an illness in the family. I am far from denying that. Most of us are aware of this responsibility and most families meet it rather well. In fact, families deliver more than 80% of the long-term care in this country, almost always at great personal cost. Most of us who are a part of a family can expect to be sustained in our time of need by family members and those who love us.

But most discussions of an illness in the family talk as if responsibility were a one-way street. It is not, of course. When we become seriously ill or debilitated, we too may have to make sacrifices. To think that my loved ones must bear whatever burdens my illness, debility, or dying process might impose upon them is to reduce them to means to my well-being. And that would be immoral. Family solidarity, altruism, bearing the burden of a loved one's misfortune, and loyalty are all important virtues of families, as well. But they are all also two-way streets. . . .

A Duty to Die and the Meaning of Life

A duty to die seems very harsh, and often it would be. It is one of the tragedies of our lives that someone who wants very much to live can nevertheless have a duty to die. It is both tragic and ironic that it is precisely the very real good of family and loved ones that gives rise to this duty. Indeed, the genuine love, closeness and supportiveness of family members is a major source of this duty: we could not be such a burden if they did not care for us. Finally, there is deep irony in the fact that the very successes of our life-prolonging medicine help to create a widespread duty to die. We do not live in such a happy world that we can avoid such tragedies and ironies. We ought not to close our eyes to this reality or pretend that it just doesn't exist. We ought not to minimize the tragedy in any way.

And yet, a duty to die will not always be as harsh as we might assume. If I love my family, I will want to protect them and their lives. I will want not to make choices that compromise their futures. Indeed, I can easily imagine that I might want to avoid compromising their lives more than I would want anything else. I must also admit that I am not necessarily giving up so much in giving up my life: the conditions that give rise to a duty to die would usually already have compromised the quality of the life I am required to end. In any case, I personally must confess that at age fifty-six, I have already lived a very good life, albeit not yet nearly as long a life as I would like to have.

We fear death too much. Our fear of death has led to a massive assault on it. We still crave after virtually any life-prolonging technology that we might conceivably be able to produce. We still too often feel morally impelled to prolong life—virtually any form of life—as long as possible. As if the best death is the one that can be put off longest.

We do not even ask about meaning in death, so busy are we with trying to postpone it. But we will not conquer death by one day developing a technology so magnificent that no one will have to die. Nor can we conquer death by postponing it ever longer. We can conquer death only by finding meaning in it.

Although the existence of a duty to die does not hinge on this, recognizing such a duty would go some way toward recovering meaning in death. 1) Paradoxically, it would restore dignity to those who are seriously ill or dying. 2) It would affirm the connections required to give life (and death) meaning. I close now with a few words on each of these points.

First, recognizing a duty to die affirms my agency and also my moral agency. I can still do things that make an important difference in the lives of my loved ones. Moreover, the fact that I still have responsibilities keeps me within the community of moral agents. My illness or debility has not reduced me to a mere moral patient (to use the language of the philosophers). Though it may not be the whole story, surely [philosopher Immanuel] Kant was onto something important when he claimed that human dignity rests on the capacity for moral agency within a community of those who respect the demands of morality.

> **" If I end my life to spare the futures of my loved ones, I testify in my death that I am connected to them. "**

By contrast, surely there is something deeply insulting in a medicine and a bioethics that would ask only what I want (or would have wanted) when I become ill. To treat me as if I had no moral responsibilities when I am ill or debilitated implies that my condition has rendered me morally incompetent. Only small children, the demented or insane, and those totally lacking in the capacity to act are free from moral duties. There is dignity, then, and a kind of meaning in moral agency, even as it forces extremely difficult decisions upon us.

Secondly, recovering meaning in death requires an affirmation of connections. If I end my life to spare the futures of my loved ones, I testify in my death that I am connected to them.

It is because I love and care for precisely these people (and I know they care for me) that I wish not to be such a burden to them. By contrast, a life in which I am free to choose whatever I want for myself is a life unconnected to others. A bioethics that would treat me as if I had no serious moral responsibilities does what it can to marginalize, weaken, or even destroy my connections with others.

But life without connection is meaningless. The individualistic fantasy, though occasionally liberating, is deeply destructive. When life is good and vitality seems unending, life itself and life lived for yourself may seem quite sufficient. But if not life, certainly death without connection is meaningless. If you are only for yourself, all you have to care about as your life draws to a close is yourself and your life. Everything you care about will then perish in your death. And that—the end of everything you care about—is precisely the total collapse of meaning. We can, then, find meaning in death only through a sense of connection with something that will survive our death.

This need not be connections with other people. Some people are deeply tied to land (e.g., the family farm), to nature, or to a transcendent reality. But for most of us, the connections that sustain us are to other people. In the full bloom of life, we are connected to others in many ways—through work, profession, neighborhood, country, shared faith and worship, common leisure pursuits, friendships. Even the guru meditating in isolation on his mountain top is connected to a long tradition of people united by the same religious quest.

But as we age or when we become chronically ill, connections with other people usually become more restricted. Often only ties with family and close friends remain and remain important to us. Moreover, for many of us, other connections just don't go deep enough. As [former Massachusetts governor] Paul Tsongas has reminded us, "when it comes time to die, no one says, 'I wish I had spent more time at the office.'"

If I am correct, death is so difficult for us partly because our sense of community is so weak. Death seems to wipe out everything when we can't fit it into the lives of those who live on. A death motivated by the desire to spare the futures of my loved ones might well be a better death for me than the one I would get as a result of opting to continue my life as long as there is any pleasure in it for me. Pleasure is nice, but it is meaning that matters.

I don't know about others, but these reflections have helped me. I am now more at peace about facing a duty to die. Ending my life if my duty required might still be difficult. But for me, a far greater horror would be dying all alone or stealing the futures of my loved ones in order to buy a little more time for myself. I hope that if the time comes when I have a duty to die, I will recognize it, encourage my loved ones to recognize it too, and carry it out bravely.

8

People Should Accept Death as Inevitable

Richard John Neuhaus

Richard John Neuhaus, who became a Roman Catholic priest in 1991, is the founder of the Institute for Religion and Public Life and editor in chief of its journal First Things.

For most people death is the antithesis of all that is good, and should, therefore, be avoided, delayed, and denied. In a culture fixated on youth and health, death is an unpopular topic. In spite of our attempts to keep death at bay, however, death is inevitable. Current trends in learning how to cope with dying or in analyzing the various stages of grief do not address the reality of death's inevitability. Rather than trying to avoid death, people must learn to accept it.

We are born to die. Not that death is the purpose of our being born, but we are born toward death, and in each of our lives the work of dying is already underway. The work of dying well is, in largest part, the work of living well. Most of us are at ease in discussing what makes for a good life, but we typically become tongue-tied and nervous when the discussion turns to a good death. As children of a culture radically, even religiously, devoted to youth and health, many find it incomprehensible, indeed offensive, that the word "good" should in any way be associated with death. Death, it is thought, is an unmitigated evil, the very antithesis of all that is good.

Death is to be warded off by exercise, by healthy habits, by medical advances. What cannot be halted can be delayed, and what cannot forever be delayed can be denied. But all our progress and all our protest notwithstanding, the mortality rate holds steady at 100 percent.

Death is the most everyday of everyday things. It is not simply that thousands of people die every day, that thousands will die this day, although that too is true. Death is the warp and woof of existence in the ordinary, the quotidian, the way things are. It is the horizon against which we get up in the morning and go to bed at night, and the next morning we awake to find the horizon has drawn closer. From the twelfth-century Enchiridion Leonis comes the nighttime prayer of children of all ages: "Now I lay me down to sleep, I pray thee Lord my soul to keep; if I should die before I wake, I pray thee Lord my soul to take." Every going to sleep is a little death, a rehearsal for the real thing.

Such is the generality, the warp and woof of everyday existence with which the wise have learned to live. But then our wisdom is shattered, not by a sudden awareness of the generality but by the singularity of a death—by the death of someone we love with a love inseparable from life. Or it is shattered by the imminent prospect of our own dying. With the cultivated complacency of the mass murderer that he was, Joseph Stalin observed, "One death is a tragedy; a million deaths is a statistic." The generality is a buffer against both guilt and sorrow. It is death in the singular that shatters all we thought we knew about death. It is death in the singular that turns the problem of death into the catastrophe of death. Thus the lamentation of [twentieth-century Catholic philosopher] Dietrich von Hildebrand: "I am filled with disgust and emptiness over the rhythm of everyday life that goes relentlessly on—as though nothing had changed, as though I had not lost my precious beloved!". . .

Death Is Not Something to Be Analyzed or Ritualized

Death and dying has become a strangely popular topic. "Support groups" for the bereaved crop up all over. How to "cope" with dying is a regular [topic] on television talk shows. It no doubt has something to do with the growing number of old people in the population. "So many more people seem to die these days," remarked my elderly aunt as she looked over the obituary columns in the local daily. Obituaries routinely include medical details once thought to be the private business of the family. Every evening without fail, at least in our cities, the television news carries a "sob shot" of relatives who have lost someone in an accident or crime. "And how did you feel when you saw she was dead?" The intrusiveness is shameless, and taboos once broken are hard to put back together again.

> **//** *[Death] is the horizon against which we get up in the morning and go to bed at night, and the next morning we awake to find the horizon has drawn closer.* **//**

[Novelist] Evelyn Waugh's *The Loved One* brilliantly satirized and [author] Jessica Mitford's *The American Way of Death* brutally savaged the death industry of commercial exploitation. Years later it may be time for a similarly critical look at the psychological death industry that got underway in 1969 when Elisabeth Kübler-Ross [psychiatrist and author of the book, *On Death and Dying*] set forth her five stages of grieving—denial, anger, bargaining, depression, and acceptance. No doubt many people feel they have been helped by formal and informal therapies for bereavement and, if they feel they have been helped, they probably have been helped in some way that is not unimportant. Just being able to get through the day without cracking up is no little thing. But neither, one may suggest, is it the most important thing. I have listened to people who speak with studied, almost clinical, detail about where they are in their trek through the five stages. Death and bereavement are "processed." There are hundreds of self-help books on how to cope with death in order to get on with life. This essay is not of that genre.

A measure of reticence and silence is in order. There is a time simply to be present to death—whether one's own or that of others—without any felt urgencies about doing something about it or getting over it. The Preacher had it right: "For everything there is a season, and a time for every matter under heaven: a time to be born, and a time to die . . . a time to mourn, and a time to dance [Ecclesiastes 3]." The time of mourning should be given its due. One may be permitted to wonder about the wisdom of contemporary funeral rites that hurry to the dancing, displacing sorrow with the determined affirmation of resurrection hope, supplying a ready answer to a question that has not been given time to understand itself. One may even long for the Dies Irae [a Latin hymn on the Day of Judgment], the sequence at the old Requiem Mass. Dies irae, dies illa/Solvet saeclum in favilla/Teste David cum Sibylla: "Day of wrath and terror looming/Heaven and earth to ash consuming/Seer's and Psalmist's true foredooming."

The worst thing is not the sorrow or the loss or the heartbreak. Worse is to be encountered by death and not to be changed by the encounter. There are pills we can take to get through the experience, but the danger is that we then do not go through the experience but around it. Traditions of wisdom encourage us to stay with death a while. Among observant Jews, for instance, those closest to the deceased observe shiva [a traditional mourning period] for seven days following the death. During shiva one does not work, bathe, put on shoes, engage in intercourse, read Torah, or have his hair cut. The mourners are to behave as though they themselves had died. The first response to death is to give inconsolable grief its due. Such grief is assimilated during the seven days of shiva, and then tempered by a month of more moderate mourning. After a year all mourning is set aside, except for the praying of kaddish, the prayer for the dead, on the anniversary of the death.

> *There is a time simply to be present to death— whether one's own or that of others—without any felt urgencies about doing something about it or getting over it.*

In *The Blood of the Lamb*, [American editor and author] Peter de Vries calls us to "the recognition of how long, how very long, is the mourners' bench upon which we sit, arms linked in undeluded friendship—all of us, brief links ourselves, in the eternal pity." From the pity we may hope that wisdom has been distilled, a wisdom from which we can benefit when we take our place on the mourners' bench. Philosophy means the love of wisdom, and so some may look to philosophers in their time of loss and aloneness. [American philosopher and poet] George Santayana wrote, "A good way of testing the caliber of a philosophy is to ask what it thinks of death." What does it tell us that modern philosophy has had relatively little to say about death? [Austrian-born philosopher] Ludwig Wittgenstein wrote, "What can be said at all can be said clearly; and whereof one cannot speak thereof one must be silent." There is undoubtedly wisdom in such reticence that stands in refreshing contrast to a popular culture sated by therapeutic chatter. But those who sit, arms linked in undeluded friendship, cannot help but ask and wonder.

We Can Learn from Those Who Die

All philosophy begins in wonder, said the ancients. With exceptions, contemporary philosophy stops at wonder. We are told: don't ask, don't wonder, about what you cannot know for sure. But the most important things of everyday life we cannot know for sure. We cannot know them beyond all possibility of their turning out to be false. We order our loves and loyalties, we invest our years with meaning and our death with hope, not knowing for sure, beyond all reasonable doubt, whether we might not have gotten it wrong. What we need is a philosophy that enables us to speak truly, if not clearly, a wisdom that does not eliminate but comprehends our doubt.

A long time ago, when I was a young pastor in a very black and very poor inner-city parish that could not pay a salary, I worked part-time as chaplain at Kings County Hospital in Brooklyn. With more than three thousand beds, Kings County boasted then of being the largest medical center in the world. It seems primitive now, but thirty-five years ago not much of a fuss was made about those who were beyond reasonable hope of recovery. They were almost all poor people, and this was before Medicare or Medicaid, so it was, as we used to say, a charity hospital. They were sedated, and food was brought for those who could eat. The dying, male and female, had their beds lined up side by side in a huge ward, fifty to a hundred of them at any given time. On hot summer days and without air-conditioning, they would fitfully toss off sheets and undergarments. The scene of naked and half-naked bodies groaning and writhing was reminiscent of Dante's Purgatorio.

Hardly a twenty-four-hour stint would go by without my accompanying two or three or more people to their death. One such death is indelibly printed upon my memory. His name was Albert, a man of about seventy and (I don't know why it sticks in my mind) completely bald. That hot summer morning

I had prayed with him and read the Twenty-third Psalm. Toward evening, I went up again to the death ward—for so everybody called it—to see him again. Clearly the end was near. Although he had been given a sedative, he was entirely lucid. I put my left arm around his shoulder and together, face almost touching face, we prayed the Our Father. Then Albert's eyes opened wider, as though he had seen something in my expression. "Oh," he said, "Oh, don't be afraid." His body sagged back and he was dead. Stunned, I realized that, while I thought I was ministering to him, his last moment of life was expended in ministering to me.

There is another death that will not leave me. Charlie Williams was a deacon of St. John the Evangelist in Brooklyn. (We sometimes called the parish St. John the Mundane in order to distinguish it from St. John the Divine, the Episcopal cathedral up on Morningside Heights.) Charlie was an ever ebullient and sustaining presence through rough times. In the face of every difficulty, he had no doubt but that "Jesus going to see us through." Then something went bad in his chest, and the doctors made medically erudite noises to cover their ignorance. I held his hand as he died a painful death at age forty-three. Through the blood that bubbled up from his hemorrhaging lungs he formed his last word—very quietly, not complaining but deeply puzzled, he looked up at me and said, "Why?"

Between Albert's calm assurance and Charlie's puzzlement, who is to say which is the Christian way to die? I have been with others who screamed defiance, and some who screamed with pain, and many who just went to sleep. Typically today the patient is heavily sedated and plugged into sundry machines. One only knows that death has come when the beeping lines on the monitors go flat or the attending physician nods his head in acknowledgment of medicine's defeat. It used to be that we accompanied sisters and brothers to their final encounter. Now we mostly sit by and wait. The last moment that we are really with them, and they with us, is often hours or even many days before they die. But medical technology notwithstanding, for each one of them, for each one of us, at some point "it" happens.

9

Funeral Rituals Help the Bereaved Cope with Death

Robert Kastenbaum

Robert Kastenbaum, professor emeritus at Arizona State University, is a renowned scholar and authority on the psychology of death. He is author of the book The Psychology of Death, *and is the editor of the* Macmillan Encyclopedia of Death *and a coeditor of* The Encyclopedia of Aging and the Humanities. *He also served as editor of the* International Journal of Aging and Human Development. *His textbook* Death, Society, and the Human Experience *is now in its eighth edition. His current work is* On Our Way: The Final Passage Through Life and Death, *published by University of California Press.*

Cultural attitudes about the role of funerals have changed. In America people view death as an inconvenience, and funerals as an expensive and meaningless rite. The funeral industry has replaced the role of the family in making arrangements and preparing the body for burial, declining religious affiliation has secularized the memorial service, and increasing institutionalization of the elderly has isolated many from their personal support systems. These and other factors have resulted in a society that does not provide for the symbolic safe passage for the dead. Americans must recognize that taking care of the dead represents a vital part of their support for the living.

We can learn about a society from the questions asked as well as the answers provided. "Funerals are for the living" is a preemptory answer that often presents itself even before a question can be raised. This fast-trigger answer to an unasked question protects us from uncomfortable reflections about our beliefs and assumptions. Crawling through a convenient escape hatch, however, can be inconsistent with our responsibilities as human-service providers. We try to cultivate perspective, a readiness for reflection, and the nerve to cross into difficult territory when the situation so requires.

> **Something crucial to the survival of a society is endangered when the living are unwilling or unable to continue customs and rituals intended to regulate relationships with the dead.**

Coming to the present case, we can be more helpful to people who are facing death-related issues if we are prepared to go beyond the formulaic answer to the question, Why funerals? Echoes from the past are resonating today within a high-tech society that has been trying hard not to listen. Beneath our whiz-bang, cybernetic, palm-pilot daily whirl we still have much in common with those who confronted death long before history found an enduring voice. Our orientation must somehow take into account both the distinctive characteristics of life in the early twenty-first century and our continuing bonds with all who have experienced the loss of loved ones. We begin, then, with a retrospective view and then look at funerals in our own time. . . .

The Dead: Vulnerable and Dangerous

Early history speaks to us in the remote and fragmented language of bones, shards, tools, and burial mounds. The archaeological history of life on earth reaches farther back than written records. Bones are still being consulted by forensic investigators and remains of eminent citizens of Verona are being exhumed and analyzed more than six hundred years after their owners drew their final breaths. Furthermore, ancient documents were often devoted to the perils faced in the journey of the dead. Rituals for guiding and communicating with the dead have been at the core of virtually all world cultures. It has been suggested that the spiritual health of a society can be evaluated by the vigor with which it continues to perform its obligations to the dead. Something crucial to the survival of a society is endangered when the living are unwilling or unable to continue customs and rituals intended to regulate relationships with the dead.

Through the millennia, our ancestors performed rituals both to affirm communal bonds among the living and to secure the goodwill of the resident deities. Ritual performances instructed members in their group responsibilities, celebrated life, encouraged fertility, and offered protection from malevolent forces. In this sense, funerary rites certainly were for the living—but that was only part of the story. Funerals were for the dead, too. An outsider with a sharp pencil and a notebook might insist on separating and classifying societal practices, including the "for the living," and "for the dead." The society itself, though, was more likely to regard all these beliefs and processes as integrated within its worldview. From the insider's perspective it was obvious that the living needed to do right by the dead. Failure to carry through with postmortem obligations could provoke the wrath of the deceased as well as the gods. Moreover, the discontented dead were not only dangerous—they were also vulnerable, needing the help of the living community. Everybody—living and dead—was in it together.

> *The living had two persuasive reasons for taking good care of their dead: love and fear.*

The living had two persuasive reasons for taking good care of their dead: love and fear. Although the details of mourning customs have varied widely, people everywhere have generally sorrowed at the loss of a person dear to them. We would recognize the anguish of newly bereaved people thousands of years ago and they would recognize ours:

- We would both want to feel that our loved one is "all right," even though dead.
- We would not feel ready to serve our ties completely. There seems to be a powerful need for what has become known in recent years as "continuing bonds."

- And we would want—somehow—to continue to express our love and respect, and to keep something of that person with us.

Today, a widow might not choose to convert her husband's jawbone into a necklace or his skull into a lime-pot, but this worked for the Trobriand Islanders as they preserved and transformed anatomical artifacts to serve as generational hand-me-downs in memory of those who had come before. Perhaps the islanders would have made DVDs from the family album had this technology been available—or perhaps the "real thing" was to be preferred in any event. Whatever the particular practice, the living could not rest easy until the departed spirits were likewise settled into their spiritual or symbolic estate. . . .

> **"** *Funeral and memorial services eventually were held without the bodies when it became clear that the remains would never be recovered and identified.* **"**

Horrible nightmares have afflicted people in many times and places when they have failed to assist the dead in their passage to the next life. It's the difference between a comforting visit from the spirit of a deceased loved one and the uneasy sense of being haunted. An example of epic proportions occurred during the prime killing years of the Black Death in fourteenth-century North Africa, Asia, and Europe. The dead sometimes outnumbered the living, who, frightened and struggling for their own survival, often had to forgo ritual and dump bodies into large burial pits or crowded shallow graves. Survivor stress included the fear that their own souls had been condemned for the failure to provide the proper rituals and services. It is even possible that the fourteenth century's intensified violence and episodes of mass psychotic behavior owed something to this violation of the implicit contract between the living and the dead.

Ground Zero: A Kind of Limbo

The abundant examples in our own time include the repeated television images of "first responders" to the attacks on the

World Trade Center on September 11, 2001, as they worked desperately, first to rescue living victims and then to uncover human remains in Ground Zero rubble. Few would have difficulty in understanding the urgent (and, unfortunately, unrewarded) efforts at rescue. The great determination to recover the dead, however, was probably instructive to a public that had become accustomed to a more pragmatic and functionalistic approach. The assumption that "the dead are just dead" was forcefully contradicted. The victims were no longer alive, but they were not yet "safely dead," if the phrase be permitted. Both the victims and their families were in a kind of a limbo—actually, in a *limbic* zone between one identity and another. Rites-of-passage theory conceives of life as a sequence of many smaller journeys within the larger tour of the total course of existence. The theory often emphasizes the vulnerability of people who have moved from their previous secure status but have not yet reached their next destination or haven.

> *Studies have suggested that older adults tend to find more comfort and meaning in funerals, but it is an open question whether 'the new aged' of each generation will continue to find as much value.*

Both the September 11 victims and the stricken families were trapped in this nowhere zone, and there was no certain endpoint at which this painful situation would be resolved. Families who had lost a member in the September 11 disaster felt they could not really start to go on with their lives until the dead had been "brought home" in some meaningful sense of the term. Funeral and memorial services eventually were held without the bodies when it became clear that the remains would never be recovered and identified. In these and many other instances, the living have expressed their need to do all that should and could be done for the dead. For the living really to get back to life (as best they could) required that the dead also be given the opportunity to move securely to their destination on time's relentless caravan. Such circumstances illustrate how simplistic it would be to insist that funerals were either just for the living or the dead.

The Inconvenient Dead in a Cloud of Confusion

In our times, the "why funerals?" question is sometimes prompted by a feeling that the dead have become an inconvenience. Funerals are merely vestigial rites that drain our precious time, money, and energy. Funerals are usually depressing affairs anyway, not that much help even to the living. We can hardly wait until they are over and then the dead are still dead, so what's been accomplished?

This view does not yet seem to be dominant in North American society but has become increasingly evident since our transformation from an agrarian nation in which most people stayed pretty much in place and the church was a cornerstone of communal life. "Deathways" have moved slowly and reluctantly along with the times as we have become a technologically enhanced land where change of address, job, and partner have become normative. Furthermore, along with other developed nations, we have achieved a significantly longer average life expectancy. Funerals less often become a gathering for sorrowing parents as their young children are laid to rest; more often the mourners are adult children who are paying their respects to a long-lived parent.

> *People who have lived essentially solitary lives or become institutional residents have a high probability of exiting this life through the backdoor with minimal attention.*

There are also signs of generational differences in the importance attached to funerals and memorial services. People still make sentimental journeys to visit family burial places. With disconcerting frequency, however, the remembered neighborhoods of their childhood have been altered beyond recognition or acceptance. Many burial places, whether in churchyards, woodland fields, or town cemeteries, have deteriorated for lack of upkeep, or have even been obliterated by the forces of change. It is understandable that some family members would rather keep their memories than face such sad prospects. The dazzling phenomenon of Americans in motion has dispersed many families who "in the old days" would have been regularly popping into each other's kitchens on a regular basis. Many families do remain emotionally connected and take advantage of up-to-date communication technology. Nevertheless, it is often a physical and financial strain to travel to bedside and funeral. Studies have suggested that older adults tend to find more comfort and meaning in funerals, but it is an open question whether "the new aged" of each generation will continue to find as much value. Even years ago I would often hear from elders that it would be a shame to waste money on "funeral stuff." One of the unforgettable comments came from the resident of a geriatric hospital:

> You come here and everybody thinks you're already dead. Tell the truth: I knew I was near dead before. Every time you walk in a store and wait and nobody sees you. . . . Just being old is just almost like being dead. Then, here. Then, dead. Who's going to care? Make a fuss? Not them. Not me.

We can hardly be surprised if people socialized within a gerophobic society should themselves internalize negative attitudes and decide that their deaths as well as their lives are undeserving of attention. Others, though, rally against the ageism and try to secure a dignified and appropriate funeral for themselves. The depressive surrender and the anxious seeking are differential responses to the same underlying concern: that a long life will receive an exit stamp of "Invalid: Discard. Shelf life expired."

Why Funerals Today?

Funerals traditionally have provided both an endpoint and a starting point. The passage from life to death is certified as complete, so the survivors now can turn to their recovery and renewal. The effectiveness of funerals to achieve this bridging purpose can be compromised, however, by some characteristics of our times. For example, many folkways involved intensive family participation in preparing the body and the funeral arrangements. . . . In general, though, the preparation phase has passed to the funeral industry with the result that family mourners less often have the complete sense of release because of their limited involvement before the funeral. Furthermore, rapid socio-technological change has reduced intergenerational consensus on the value of the funeral process. One cannot assume that multiple-generation families will share priorities and expectations.

Another challenge to the social and spiritual value of funerals [is] an increase in the frequency of "funerals of the unaffiliated." More than a third of the U.S. population do not claim membership in a religious congregation. Religious officials confirm that they are being called upon more often to participate in such funerals in which families request that the religious service be "toned down."

> *" The funeral process today is caught up within the broader matrix of social change. "*

I have noticed a parallel trend that might be called "funerals of the disengaged." People who have outlived—or, over time, drifted away from—their personal support systems are more likely to receive only perfunctory services. Those who would have felt a strong emotional link or at least a powerful sense of obligation have already passed from that person's life. People who have lived essentially solitary lives or become institutional residents have a high probability of exiting this life through the backdoor with minimal attention. Such an exit was a frequent occurrence within institutional settings where many residents seemed to have been forgotten or disregarded by the larger community and the facility itself was locked into a death-avoidance pattern. A funeral process that does not celebrate the life, mourn the passing, or provide symbolic safe passage through the journey of the dead—what else can we expect when the individual has been progressively disvalued through the years?

It is understandable that funerals might be disvalued if they seem to have lost their inner connection to the values and meanings that guide our lives. It is that inner connection that makes a difference between empty ritual and participation in an event that is both universal and deeply personal. To ask "Why funerals?" may sound like a rejection of the whole process. Most often, though, the question expresses a search for renewal of the inner connection between how we live and how we die.

That search is now taking a variety of forms. People who are uncomfortable with the familiar words, symbols, and gestures of mainstream religion are nevertheless finding ways to incorporate spiritual considerations into the funeral process.

The "postmodern funeral" may include such elements as a candle-lighting ceremony and improvised memorials, music, and eulogies that are somehow special to the particular people involved. New partnerships are developing between those funeral directors who are open to change and those families who are determined that the funeral process represent their own way of life. . . .

The funeral process today is caught up within the broader matrix of social change. Some of the negatives have already been identified. To these must be added that narrow construction of human life that embraces youth and material success but recoils from the specter of loss and limits. Where this attitudinal climate prevails, it is tempting to reject funerals because we are exposed there to the uncomfortable reminders of aging and death. Nevertheless, it remains as true today as ever that "taking good care of the dead" is a vital part of a society's support for the living. . . .

Yes, funerals can take the form of dysfunctional vestiges if we let them go that way. Another choice is available to us, though. We can recognize that the funeral process offers an opportunity to reach deep into our understanding and values. Perhaps our society today does not offer the clearest and firmest guide to comprehension of life and death. Perhaps it is up to us, then, to review our own beliefs about the meanings of growth and loss, youth and age, life and death—and to listen carefully to the beliefs of those to whom we offer service.

10

Alternatives to the Traditional Funeral Can Comfort the Bereaved

Nancy Rommelmann

Nancy Rommelmann's articles have appeared in the New York Times Magazine, *the* Los Angeles Times, *and the* LA Weekly.

Only in the last century has the responsibility of caring for the dead been passed on to professionals. Before that, the loved one's family prepared the bodies of the deceased at home and buried them on family property. The $20-billion-a-year funeral industry is not only costly, but it contributes to American society's fear of death. An alternative-death movement in America is trying to address these problems by developing rituals that do not involve the funeral industry. Proponents of this movement encourage home preparation of the body without the assistance of an undertaker, and suggest green burials in which the body can decompose naturally. These practices promote healing among the bereaved and are environmentally friendly as well. Proponents hope that these grassroots efforts will not only help people heal more quickly after their loss, but will also become a powerful conservation tool to save millions of acres of land.

For centuries in America, we tended to our dead. People died at home, and relatives prepared the body, laid it out in the parlor and sat by as callers paid final respects. The body was buried in the family cemetery, if there was one, or on the back 40; pieties were spoken, and life went on until the next person died. Death, if not a welcome visitor, was a familiar one. This changed, incrementally, during the Civil War, when others were paid to undertake the job of transporting the bodies of soldiers killed far from home; this is when formaldehyde as an embalming agent was first used. But it was only 100 years ago that we began routinely to hand over our dead to the undertakers. Soon the gravely ill as well were deemed too taxing, and moved to hospitals to die. Within decades, what had for millennia been familial responsibilities were appropriated by professionals.

"People think we're not emotionally capable, let alone physically capable, of carrying this out," says Jerri Lyons. "Well, what were we doing before when we weren't supposedly able to take care of people?"

Lyons is making tea in the small cottage she shares with her husband in a leafy glade in Sebastopol [California]. Bookshelves overspill, a computer is crammed into a nook and there is no room for a dining set, so Lyons sets the teacups on her massage table, which, in any case, is multipurpose.

"We use it to turn people during seminars," she says. "We use it for reiki [touch therapy], and we also lend it to families that want to have a showing at home."

What she means by "a showing" is a wake. But Lyons, a 57-year-old former Costco rep and café owner, is not an undertaker, or, in her euphemistic parlance, a "well-intended grief choreographer." In fact, there is as yet no title for what she does, which is to teach people about their right to a home funeral and how to prepare the body for it.

> *This country's 'death-denying tradition'. . . is not merely costly but corrosive to body and spirit, to land and communities.*

There's an alternative-death movement fomenting in Northern California, one that leaves the funeral industry out of the picture altogether. Proponents of home funerals and of green burials, wherein bodies are interred in natural environments and in ways that promote decomposition, insist that this country's "death-denying tradition," in Lyons' term, is not merely costly but corrosive to body and spirit, to land and communities. Fear and doubt, they say, crept into the space left when we handed death to others, and our attendant helplessness supports the multibillion-dollar death-care industry. And they know, even if we don't yet, just how badly we want to bury our own dead.

> **" The body can lie in state at home for up to three days, and perhaps longer, provided measures are taken within the first six to 12 hours. "**

"We're always afraid of the unknown, until we've been exposed to it and seen that it isn't frightening," says Lyons, proffering several fat albums containing photographs of former clients: dark-haired Donna, who stenciled her own casket before dying of a brain tumor at 32; Bernd, who also died of cancer, lying in bed, wearing a prayer shawl, his mouth curled in an easy smile. There is nothing ghoulish or grotesque about the images; there is neither rictus nor putrefaction. Instead, there's a 3-year-old in foot-pajamas peering at Aunt Donna, lain out after death in her own bedroom.

There's also a picture of Carolyn Whiting, who died suddenly of respiratory failure in 1994 and whose friends, Lyons says, "were simply not ready to let her go."

Is It Legal?

It turned out that they did not have to. Convening at Whiting's home the night of her death, Lyons and others learned that she had left instructions as to how she wanted to be cared for. "She did not want to be turned over to a mortuary," Lyons says, "but rather wanted her friends to bring her body home if she was in the hospital, and prepare her body."

Lyons admits that they were caught off guard. "I don't think this would have occurred to us at all," she says. "We, like everyone else I talk to about home funerals, would have asked, 'Is that legal?'"

Home preparation of the deceased, without an undertaker's involvement, is legal in every state but four. Today there are books (such as Lyons' "Creating Home Funerals" and Lisa Carlson's "Caring for the Dead: Your Final Act of Love") that give detailed instructions in after-death care. At the time, Whiting's friends winged it: They took her body home, bathed and perfumed her, picked out clothing, held a wake, and then loaded Whiting into a van and drove her to the crematory.

"It was so helpful to us, to deal with our shock and our grief, and in such a loving, beautiful way to celebrate her life," says Lyons, who went on to found Final Passages, a nonprofit educational program, and Home and Family Funerals, a service wherein Lyons is paid as a "death-midwife," helping the dying and their families with everything from preparing the body to filing paperwork. She works on a sliding scale, but says a full cremation with her facilitation could cost $750. She estimates that in the last 10 years she's helped more than 250 people "pass over."

"A person, their body doesn't immediately look white as a ghost, or change rapidly," Lyons says. "People think they're going to start decomposing instantly. And that's not so."

> *Feeling the body lose its warmth, seeing the tension leave the face, being present for the transition from life to death . . . helps us to accept that the person is gone.*

As she teaches in seminars around the country, the body can lie in state at home for up to three days, and perhaps longer, provided measures are taken within the first six to 12 hours. The body should be well washed, especially the genitals, with warm, soapy water; the abdomen should be pressed to expel any waste. After the body is dried and dressed, ice (preferably dry but regular will do), which has been wrapped in grocery bags and then cloth, should be placed beneath the torso to keep the organs cool, as these are the first parts of the body to break down. The body should be kept in a cool room. If the person dies with his mouth open, which can be disconcerting to visitors, a scarf may be looped beneath the chin and tied around the head until the mouth sets shut. Similarly, eyes may be closed by gently weighing them down with small bags filled with rice or sand. The casket can be decorated, and a memorial display set up, plain or fancy. One family Lyons helped watched a video with their departed father that he'd rented but had not had a chance to see;

another put hiking boots on dad and wheeled him into the woods for a final "hiking trip to heaven."

These people were able to take a deep breath and do what needed to be done. Others need hand-holding. Lyons recently helped a family whose belief in anthroposophy (the philosophy of Rudolf Steiner) dictated that the father's body be kept at home for three days, surrounded by loved ones, read to and cared for. This frightened his teenage daughter.

> **"** *Final dispositions typically cost $8,000, though [they] can easily run to $10,000, $20,000 or more.* **"**

"She did not come in the room as we were bathing him," Lyons says, "but eventually she came in and started asking questions, and started feeling really relaxed and comfortable." So comfortable that a while later she had her friends over. "They were in the other room, talking and being normal teenagers. It was all a part of family life."

Feeling the body lose its warmth, seeing the tension leave the face, being present for the transition from life to death, Lyons says, helps us to accept that the person is gone. "The actual doing does help, because you're moving through your grief with a process, a ritual," she says. "You're present to it not just with your mind but with your senses. . . . You're not escaping, or pretending it didn't happen, or getting busy doing something else."

Grassroots Revolt

Northern California was the site of an earlier revolt against the funeral industry, when Oakland resident Jessica Mitford wrote her scathing 1963 exposé, "The American Way of Death." In updating the book for a revised edition published posthumously in 1998, Mitford found that, though consumers had put the brakes on burials, they were still being taken for a ride. "Cremation, once the best hope for a low-cost simple getaway, has become increasingly expensive," she wrote in her new introduction. "[M]orticians are fast developing techniques for upgrading this procedure into a full-fig funeral."

The "full-fig" or fancy-dress funeral in America includes embalming, whether or not one chooses cremation, so the body will have a lifelike appearance in its coffin, which will be metal. After the viewing, those who choose cremation will be transferred to a burnable container and their ashes transferred to an urn, such as the gold-plated Olympus model that Forest Lawn Memorial Parks and Mortuaries sells for $5,000. Those being buried will have their coffin placed in a concrete vault to ensure that the ground cover does not buckle, thus maintaining the putting-green uniformity of most cemeteries. Or vaults and urns may be placed in a mausoleum, for which there is a perpetual-care fee. These final dispositions typically cost $8,000, though can easily run to $10,000, $20,000 or more.

"If you ask people, they don't want any of this stuff," says Joe Sehee as he speed-hikes up a shady path in Mill Valley. "Half of what they spend money on is because they think they have to because it's required by law, mainly caskets and embalming fluid. That just angers me so much, because that's really some toxic stuff that no one should be exposed to, let alone put in the ground. And it doesn't serve any purpose!"

> *[When] the AARP website polled readers, asking: 'Which type of burial is most appealing?' . . . 70.4% . . . chose green burial.*

Sehee reaches a crest on the 32-acre property known as Fernwood and takes in the view: the Golden Gate National Recreation Area, and a necklace of multimillion-dollar homes on a nearby ridge. This is prime Marin County real estate, for which one of Sehee's partners in Fernwood paid $495,000 in 2003, a figure that will no doubt make developers keen. But the Fernwoodians do not plan to build on the land, and couldn't even if they wanted to, because there are bodies buried beneath the grounds of this former cemetery. They plan to bury more.

Fernwood is the nation's second commercial "green" cemetery, which means only natural burial techniques are used: no embalming fluid; biodegradable burial containers such as wood or a simple shroud; the vertical headstone replaced with a flat rock or a tree—or nothing, as a loved one's location is available by global positioning satellite. Since its opening in August,

1,000 people have requested a tour. . . .

Although Fernwood is owned outright by one of [business partner Tyler] Cassity's holdings, Sehee says they'd rather the land itself be owned by a nonprofit such as the National Audubon Society, or a government agency such as the Park Service, any organization with a mandate if not the money to protect land and wildlife. "Think of another idea where you can generate money by having land stay fallow," he says. "Our vision is to sort of be concessionaires, almost like the inverse of mining. Instead of paying for extraction rights, we're paying for insertion rights, but then we have money set aside to do ecological restoration and keep the land up forever. Then we have this for-profit management that operates the facility, digs the holes, builds the trails, markets the facility and moves on as this thing fills up. We can use the concept to, hopefully, restore other land. Our goal is a million acres over the next 30 years."

Sehee nods at the homes across the canyon. "Guess who some of the first customers will be to buy this property?" he asks. "All those people who want to preserve the ridge top, who live here. Those are the people who've been approaching us."

As if to illustrate his point, a family and their dogs pass by. They may be folks from the area out for a weekend walk, as Fernwood is open to the public, or they may be clients picking out their final resting spots, which they can mark with little flags.

"The people [we're] talking to are in their 40s and 50s who would never prearrange, but they know this place is going to be filled up in five or six years," says Sehee. "They also know that if they help do this, it's enlightened self-interest—they're keeping the space open for their community. Mrs. Jones is keeping her property value up by buying space to be buried here."

A Growing Trend

It's not just Mrs. Jones who's interested. When an article about Ramsey Creek Preserve appeared in the July/August 2004 issue of the *AARP* [American Association of Retired Persons] *Bulletin,* the AARP website polled readers, asking: "Which type of burial is most appealing?" Only 8.1% wanted a traditional cemetery burial; 18.6% picked cremation, while 2.9% went for "exotic burial," such as being shot into space. The rest—70.4%—chose green burial.

Which is not surprising, considering that a sizable number of AARP's 35 million members are baby boomers, a generation that never met a ritual it didn't want to retool. These are the folks who wrote their own marriage vows and demanded home birth and hospices, and now that they're burying parents and considering their own final arrangements, they're looking for alternatives to being pumped with chemicals that demean the body and degrade the earth, and caskets that cost as much as cars. Lawsuits filed in recent years, after the buildup of anaerobic bacteria in bodies in "sealer caskets" caused corpses to explode, forcing the liquefied remains to flow down the fronts of mausoleum crypts, have done similarly little to endear them to the industry.

> *[Baby boomers are] looking for alternatives to being pumped with chemicals that demean the body and degrade the earth, and caskets that cost as much as cars.*

"Universally, almost all Americans are dissatisfied with death-care options," Sehee says. "This article in AARP came out, and we realized it's religious traditionalists, it's conservatives, it's outdoors enthusiasts. Evangelical Christians love the shroud burial concept. It's obviously been part of the Jewish tradition, the Bahai tradition. It's the way most cultures buried their own until 130 years ago."

Although one does not imagine that there was a whole lot of profit in the graveyard business back in 1875, funeral arrangements and cemeteries currently generate $11 billion a year in revenue, according to the National Funeral Directors Assn., though numbers vary widely, with some estimates as high as $20 billion. The industry is dominated by just three conglomerates—Service Corp. International, Alderwoods (formerly the Loewen Group) and Stewart Enterprises.

Robyn Sadowsky, a director for corporate communication at Service Corp. International, says the traditional funeral industry is well aware of the alt-death trend. After directing inquiries to a few industry websites (where there is no information on either green or natural burial), she says the 1,800 funeral homes in the SCI network have a sole mandate: "Our role as funeral care providers is to celebrate the life of the person who has passed on, and to do it in a way that they would have liked, as well as their family."

She mentions several recent funerals that were far from traditional, such as one that included a procession of vintage cars, and another in which a person's ashes rode to the cemetery in the sidecar of a Harley-Davidson. She also mentions cremation "wreaths" that, when tossed on the water, slowly release the ashes.

And if, say, a woman went to an SCI funeral home and requested that her husband not be embalmed and casketed, but simply wrapped in a shroud and buried green?

"We would try to accommodate that," Sadowsky says, "but you have to think, what are the shroud regulations in that state? Where is the closest green cemetery? Are there refrigeration issues? There are legal and health considerations, and we have to look into all of those. A shroud and a green burial may sound dignified, and respectful of the environment, and everything the person wanted, but what do we have to do to accommodate that wish?"

Sehee is skeptical. "There's this notion of socially disruptive technology or innovation," he says. "These are ideas that completely revolutionize industries that the industries weren't interested in, because you're dealing with lower margins and problem customers. You're talking about taking away all their opportunities to make money on floral arrangements and big headstones and $7,000 caskets—why would they want to get involved in that?"

> " The traditional funeral industry is well aware of the alt-death trend. "

Not that it's cheap to buy at Fernwood. The least expensive burial of "cremains" is $1,000, burial of a body is $3,000, and all interments require a one-time 10% endowment fee to preserve and restore the land. Prime spots on the property can fetch three times as much. But it's still considerably less than at Forest Lawn, where a mid-range casket alone costs more than $9,000.

"Our bet is that this is the future, this is the way people are going to want to be buried," says Sehee. "You'll probably see a lot of green-washing [in the funeral industry]. You'll see people say they're doing green burials, and there's a couple of acres out back where you don't have to have a casket and use embalming fluid, which is great, but they'll never do conservation."

The Future of the Funeral Industry

Dr. Billy Campbell calls late one night from South Carolina, saying he's "pretty tired," having hand-dug a grave earlier in the day. How deep should a grave be?

"You want the nutrients in the human body to get to the surface, so you don't want to dig too deep—I learned that the hard way," says Campbell, an environmentalist and medical doctor who started to see how out of whack the burying business had become when he lost his father.

The funeral director "was talking about the vault, and he said, 'It'll take 20,000 pounds per square foot,'" Campbell says. "And I can remember saying to him, 'We're trying to protect the corpse from a direct nuclear strike or a runaway tractor-trailer, but what's the point? What is it we're protecting him from?' And you know what it was? Nature. That's the thing. We don't want the body to be violated by natural processes. I thought, this is stupid, and not only that, it's wasteful."

> *We're trying to protect the corpse from a direct nuclear strike or a runaway tractor-trailer, but what's the point?*

Mary Woodsen, a member of Commemorative Nature Preserves of New York, an organization that advocates memorial nature preserves, calculated three years ago what American cemeteries inter annually in addition to bodies: 827,060 gallons of embalming fluid, 1,636,000 tons of reinforced concrete, 104,272 tons of steel, 2,700 tons of copper and bronze, and 30 million board feet of hardwoods. Although the Cremation Assn. of North America predicts the national cremation rate will rise to 35% by 2010, "people don't really actively save land when they're cremated," Campbell says, "they just don't waste land."

Campbell began to look for examples of natural burial, and found them in the tall grass prairies of Iowa and Ohio. "The most diverse places were the old pioneer cemeteries," he says.

"It wasn't deep-plowed, so the old cemeteries became some of the best areas for remnant prairies. If that's by accident, why can't we do it intentionally now and turn this into a powerful [conservation] tool? You've got a $20-billion-a-year industry, you've got baby boomers—you can create places that aren't just cemeteries but where you learn about plants, and they become these multidimensional social spaces, and, oh yeah, you can be buried there too."

> *He's . . . seen the healing that happens when the grief-stricken get their hands in the dirt.*

Campbell says that as the only doctor in the town of Westminster, he's taken some flak. "My favorite line was, 'You know, Doc, you going into the cemetery business is like a vet who got a taxidermy license and put a sign in the window that says, 'Either way, you get your dog back.'" But he's also seen the healing that happens when the grief-stricken get their hands in the dirt—as recently as this afternoon, at the burial of a 44-year-old man who died in a car accident two days before Christmas, leaving a wife and four daughters.

"If you're alienated from nature and someone dies and you fix them up like they're not really dead, and you spend a lot of money and put them in a box and put turf on top of them and make it like it never happened, that's normative," he says. "But there is this potential for people to be transformed, where you see where someone is buried, like today. . . . The pallbearers actually lower the casket into the ground, and people throw dirt on top of the casket. It's amazing when you hear the dirt bouncing off the top of the casket—people break down sometimes and will actually wail. There's one guy who was there today, he was crying and digging, crying and digging, and I think that probably was therapeutic. We had one lady who came and helped dig her mom's grave and said, 'I could be back on the couch popping Xanax with the rest of them, but I'd rather be out here doing something for Mom.'"

After the AARP article ran, Ramsey Creek Preserve received 6,000 e-mails from people asking how they could be buried this way. They were not, as Campbell expected, "my fellow granola tree-hugging hippie people."

"We bury people in overalls, playing country music and throwing cigarettes in the grave," he says. "I had one guy who was buried there who said, 'I love the woods, I just don't like environmentalists.' It wasn't an ideological thing for him. It does appeal to free-market Republicans who want to see a business do this and see people make individual choices. It appeals to people who are hard-core environmentalists. We've seen a lot of support from evangelical Christians, who are talking about the Rapture and the whole nine yards, who think this is more in keeping with what the Bible says. It's like Genesis 3:19: Dust are thou and to dust thou shall return.

"I'll be 50 years old this year," Campbell says, "and I would rather protect a million acres than make a gazillion dollars, and whatever we have to do to make that happen, that's what I'm going to do."

It may soon be happening in Southern California. In December, Campbell and Sehee met with city and cemetery officials about taking over a 1,400-acre parcel in Chatsworth, as well as several pieces of land in Orange County.

"Remember when your grandfather said, 'Just put me in a pine box'?" asks Tyler Cassity. "We're going to."

11

Talking About Death and Dying Helps Families Cope with Death

Jeff Chu

Jeff Chu of Time *magazine is an award-winning journalist who won one of two five-thousand-dollar 2004 Peter R. Weitz prizes for excellence in reporting on European affairs by a journalist under thirty-five. Amanda Bower of New York, Laura A. Locke of San Francisco, and Maggie Sieger of Chicago also contributed to this report.*

Terri Schiavo, a Florida woman who had been in a vegetative state since 1990, died on March 31, 2005, after her feeding tube was removed. Because Schiavo had not been able to communicate her wishes, it was left to family members to make medical decisions for her. Unfortunately, while her husband wanted her life support removed, her parents wanted to keep her alive. Her husband ultimately prevailed. Schiavo's case has drawn attention to the difficulties families face when loved ones do not specify their wishes about end-of-life decisions in advance. However, the Schiavo case is an exception. Rarely do families become so divided. Instead, most families are able to resolve their differences through compromise, fact-finding, and consensus. Although it helps when people take the time to prepare advance directives, it is important to note that these directives are not a panacea. Indeed, advance directives can be either ignored by doctors intent on saving lives or overruled by families whose convictions will not permit them to follow through with a patient's wishes. The lesson to be learned from the Schiavo case is the importance of family members talking about how they would like to be treated in their final days.

The saga of Terri Schiavo [the Florida woman who suffered severe brain damage in 1990], has touched many Americans directly, prompting them to relive difficult decisions they've already made or can contemplate making. That the case became so celebrated, though, is a function of its atypicality. Relatives faced with a situation like Schiavo's, in which the patient has no living will, very often differ about what to do, physicians say, but rarely do the factions become so unmovable and determined to prevail as did Schiavo's husband and parents. Instead, one side usually gives in. Will the Schiavo case change that? Though Schiavo's parents were able to go to great lengths in challenging their son-in-law's decision to let Terri die, legal experts aren't convinced this will lead to many more courtroom disputes. Rather, they expect more Americans will now make their end-of-life wishes more explicit, and evidence of that is already emerging.

Dr. Gary Johanson, medical director of the Memorial Hospice and Palliative Care Center in Santa Rosa, Calif., says that when an incapacitated patient hasn't left a living will or designated someone to make his or her medical decisions, families agree on what to do anyway in about two-thirds of the cases his center sees. When relatives quarrel, he notes, it's typically over old baggage. "Maybe one person feels estranged [from the patient] and now feels guilty if they don't try everything."

> // Who has the legal right to make decisions for an incapacitated patient varies by state but the reality of family dynamics is that those choices are often made by consensus. //

When relatives disagree, compromise almost always comes when "those who wish to terminate care accede to the wishes of those who do not," says Dr. Kenneth Prager, director of the medical-ethics committee at New York-Presbyterian Hospital/

Columbia University Medical Center. "People do not want to be looked at for the rest of their lives by other family members as having been responsible for the death of a loved one." Schiavo's husband Michael is unusual, Prager says, in his insistence on carrying out what he says were her wishes not to live in a vegetative state.

Who has the legal right to make decisions for an incapacitated patient varies by state but the reality of family dynamics is that those choices are often made by consensus.

> *Relatives often need time to sift through intense feelings and to say a long goodbye.*

Health-care professionals who frequently deal with families in those situations offer two broad pieces of advice. First, "Everybody needs to hear the same thing" about the patient's prognosis, says Bruce Ambuel, a psychologist at the Medical College of Wisconsin in Milwaukee. "Otherwise you have different people hearing different things from different specialists at different times, and it just sows the seeds of conflict." Second, family members should go on a fact-finding mission to get a sense of a patient's probable desires. "Talk to as many people as possible who may know what they would have wanted, their good friends and loved ones," says Kathy Brandt, vice president of the National Hospice and Palliative Care Organization.

Sorting Through the Options Together

The Tighe family's fact-finding mission was relatively straightforward. Three years ago, Jimmy Tighe, then 48, of Cleveland, Ohio, fell down some stairs at his father's house and was knocked unconscious. The ambulance crew accidentally threaded a breathing tube into his stomach, leaving him without oxygen for the 12-minute ride to the hospital. When his brothers were told three months later that Tighe was in a persistent vegetative state, they mentally replayed conversations they had had about death four years earlier, after another brother had been shot and killed. "We all said, 'Don't put us on any life support,'" says Keith Tighe, 41. "Jimmy said it too." Still, it has taken time for the Tighes to act, as is often the case. Only in February, after Jimmy developed pneumonia, did the brothers and their father move him into a hospice and start the procedural steps required by the center before a feeding tube can be removed. In the meantime, the Tighes visit Jimmy every day.

Relatives often need time to sift through intense feelings and to say a long goodbye. Last September [2004] the family of Jill Rudolph, 41, of Toledo, Ohio, voted 5 to 3 to remove her feeding tube. She had been in a persistent vegetative state since May, when she suffered multiple strokes. Her mother Joyce Moran voted against removal. Years ago, Moran's brother-in-law had needed six months to emerge from a coma; what if Rudolph needed that time too? The family compromised, agreeing not to take immediate action. But by November, Moran had gone through an intense period of prayer, research and discussion with the doctors and her priest. On Nov. 8, doctors removed Rudolph's feeding tube but kept her on morphine. She died on Dec. 4. "My priest advised me to do the loving thing," says Moran.

Such trials can sometimes bring families closer. Marianne Svanberg, 88, a Swede, suffered a massive stroke while visiting her granddaughter Kim Gagne in Santa Rosa, Calif., in January, setting off a bitter generational row between Svanberg's daughters and granddaughters about whether to put her on a feeding tube. At one point, recalls Gagne, 40, "my mother and I had a big blowup, right there in front of the doctor." The granddaughters prevailed, and a tube was inserted, but Svanberg's condition worsened. She died on Feb. 19, leaving a family that was mournful, says Gagne, but knit tighter and united in the belief that it was right to have given Svanberg a chance to recover. "Even the aunt who was hardest on me has become a friend," Gagne says.

> *A living will is not a panacea. 'It's a piece of paper. . . . It can't get at all those gray areas that happen every day.'*

Then there are cases like that of an Iowa social worker who had guardianship over her mother, who was in a persistent vegetative state following a reaction to iodine. After three years, the woman and her sister agreed to remove their mother's feeding tube, but they did not inform their aunts for fear the women would try to stop them. "To this day, they don't really talk to us," says the social worker.

Understanding the Limitations of Advance Directives

The burdens on a family are significantly reduced when the patient has made decisions in advance—for instance, choosing a surrogate to act on his or her behalf by filling out a durable power of attorney for health care. A living will, also known as an advance directive, helps a proxy understand the patient's wishes—and "avoids the suspicion that a family is doing something for ulterior motives," notes Prager. A living will is not a panacea. "It's a piece of paper," says Brandt. "It can't get at all those gray areas that happen every day." It may specify that no "extraordinary measures" to prolong life be taken. But are those measures defined? Is CPR extraordinary? A feeding tube? A respirator? What's more, in an emergency, doctors are consumed with saving lives. In practice, written directives often don't come up.

> *Sixty-five percent of doctors surveyed said they would not necessarily follow a living will under special circumstances, such as intrafamily conflict.*

Nor can a living will always trump a family's convictions. A study published last July in the *Archives of Internal Medicine* found that 65% of doctors surveyed said they would not necessarily follow a living will under special circumstances, such as intrafamily conflict. Prager recently consulted with the relatives of an elderly woman who had suffered a cerebral hemorrhage and was clearly going to die. Her advance directive specified that no extraordinary measures be taken to save her. But her devoutly Jewish son believed that taking his mother off a ventilator would be murder. Prager's committee, the family members, their rabbi and their doctors decided that the ventilator would extend the woman's life by a few weeks, at most. "We did not feel that her will would be significantly violated," he says. She remained on the ventilator and died soon after.

The intense coverage of Terri Schiavo's experience seems to have made many Americans think, That could be me. Jay Sekulow, chief counsel of the American Center for Law and Justice, which has worked on behalf of Schiavo's parents, doubts that their efforts will motivate more families to take conflicts to court. Instead, he says, "I think people will be much more specific in what they want their medical treatment to be." Indeed, Johanson says that at his hospice, the case is "creating fear in patients that their wishes will not be met"; many are responding by "getting things down on paper." Keith Tighe says he and his brothers have reacted to the news by getting advance directives. A *Time* poll [in March 2005] found that 69% of those surveyed who do not have a living will said the Schiavo case had made them think about getting one, or at least talking with their family about how they would like to be treated in their final days.

Organizations to Contact

The editors have compiled the following list of organizations concerned with the issues debated in this book. The descriptions are derived from materials provided by the organizations. All have publications or information available for interested readers. The list was compiled on the date of publication of the present volume; the information provided here may change. Be aware that many organizations take several weeks or longer to respond to inquiries, so allow as much time as possible.

American Hospice Foundation
2120 L St. NW, Suite 200, Washington, DC 20037
(202) 223-0204 • fax: (202) 223-0208
e-mail: ahf@americanhospice.org
Web site: www.americanhospice.org

The mission of American Hospice Foundation is to improve access to quality hospice care through public education, professional training, and advocacy on behalf of consumers. The foundation supports programs that serve the needs of terminally ill and grieving individuals of all ages. It advances hospice concepts by training school professionals who work with grieving students; educating employers and managers about the needs of grieving employees; creating tools to help hospices reach out to their communities; promoting improved hospice benefits in managed care organizations; and initiating research on consumer needs and preferences in end-of-life care.

American Medical Association (AMA)
515 N. State St., Chicago, IL 60610
(800) 621-8335
Web site: www.ama-assn.org

Founded in 1847, the AMA is the primary professional association of physicians in the United States. It disseminates information concerning medical breakthroughs, medical and health legislation, educational standards for physicians, and other issues concerning medicine and health care. It opposes physician-assisted suicide. The AMA operates a library and offers many publications, including its weekly journal *JAMA*, the weekly newspaper *American Medical News*, and journals covering specific medical specialties.

American Society of Law, Medicine, and Ethics
765 Commonwealth Ave., Suite 1634, Boston, MA 02215
(617) 262-4990 • fax: (617) 437-7596
e-mail: info@aslme.org • Web site: www.aslme.org

The society's members include physicians, attorneys, health care administrators, and others interested in the relationship between law, medicine, and ethics. The organization has an information clearinghouse and a library, and it acts as a forum for discussion of issues such as euthanasia and assisted suicide. It publishes the quarterlies *American Journal of Law and Medicine* and *Journal of Law, Medicine, and Ethics;* the newsletter *ASLME Briefings;* and books such as *Legal and Ethical Aspects of Treating Critically and Terminally Ill Patients.*

Center for Loss and Life Transition
3735 Broken Bow Rd., Fort Collins, CO 80526
(970) 226-6050 • (800) 922-6051
e-mail: wolfelt@centerforloss.com • Web site: www.centerforloss.com

The Center for Loss and Life Transition is a private organization dedicated to furthering the understanding of the complex set of emotions called grief. Its mission is to help both the bereaved and their caregivers by serving as their educational liaison and professional forum. The center accomplishes its mission through a combination of workshops and publications. It is also an educational and training center for bereavement caregivers.

Center for Thanatology Research & Education
391 Atlantic Ave., Brooklyn, NY 11217-1701
(718) 858-3026 • fax: (718) 852-1846
e-mail: thanatology@pipeline.com • Web site: www.thanatology.org

The Center for Thanatology Research & Education is a nonprofit small press, library, museum, resource center, and mail-order bookseller that handles books, media, and periodicals on one major subject: the study of mortality.

Compassion in Dying
6312 SW Capitol Hwy., Suite 415, Portland, OR 97239
(503) 221-9556 • fax: (503) 228-9160
e-mail: info@compassionindying.org
Web site: www.compassionindying.org

Compassion in Dying provides information, counseling, and emotional support to terminally ill patients and their families, including information and counseling about intensive pain management, comfort or hospice care, and death-hastening methods. It promotes the view that terminally ill patients who seek to hasten their deaths should not have to die alone because their loved ones fear prosecution if they are found present. Compassion in Dying does not promote suicide but condones hastening death as a last resort when all other possibilities have been exhausted and when suffering is intolerable. It publishes the quarterly newsletter *Connections* and several pamphlets on intensive pain management and on coping with the death of a loved one. Advance directive forms for all states can be downloaded from the Compassion in Dying Web site.

Death with Dignity
1818 N St. NW, Suite 450, Washington, DC 20036
(503) 228-4415 (344-6489) • fax: (503) 228-7454
e-mail: info@deathwithdignity.org
Web site: www.deathwithdignity.org

Death with Dignity promotes a comprehensive, humane, responsive system of care for terminally ill patients. Its members believe that a dying patient's choices should be given the utmost respect and consideration. The center serves as an information resource for the public and the media, and promotes strategies for advancing a responsive system of care for terminally ill patients on educational, legal, legislative, and public-policy fronts. It publishes several fact sheets, including *Misconceptions in the Debate on Death with Dignity, The Situation in Florida, Dying in the U.S.A.: A Call for Public Debate,* and *The Issue: From the Individual's Perspective,* all of which are available in an information package by request.

End of Life Choices
PO Box 101810, Denver, CO 80250-1810
(800) 247-7421 • fax: (303) 639-1224
e-mail: info@endoflifechoices.org
Web site: www.endoflifechoices.org

Founded as the Hemlock Society in 1980, End of Life Choices has one core goal: to assure freedom of choice at the end of life. It advocates for the right of terminally ill, mentally competent adults to hasten death under careful safeguards. The organization believes that each person is entitled to choose within the law both how to live and how to die. The organization provides education, information, and advice about choices at the end of life and options available to the terminally ill.

Euthanasia Research and Guidance Organization (ERGO)
24829 Norris Ln., Junction City, OR 97448-9559
(541) 998-1873 • fax: (541) 998-1873
e-mail: ergo@efn.org • Web site: www.finalexit.org

ERGO provides information and research findings on physician-assisted dying to persons who are terminally or hopelessly ill and wish to end their suffering. Its members counsel dying patients and develop ethical, psychological, and legal guidelines to help them and their physicians make life-ending decisions. The organization's publications include *Deciding to Die: What You Should Consider* and *Assisting a Patient to Die: A Guide for Physicians.*

Funeral Consumers Alliance
33 Patchen Rd., South Burlington, Vermont 05403
(800) 765-0107
e-mail: info@funerals.org • Web site: www.funerals.org

The Funeral Consumers Alliance works to promote the affordability, dignity, and simplicity of funeral rites and memorial services. The alliance believes that every person should have the opportunity to choose the type of funeral or memorial service he or she desires. It provides information on body and organ donation and on funeral costs, and it lobbies for reform of funeral regulations at the state and federal levels. The alliance's publications include the end-of-life planning guide *Before I Go, You Should Know* and the quarterly *FCA Newsletter.*

Growth House
(415) 863-3045
e-mail: info@growthhouse.org • Web site: www.growthhouse.org

Growth House provides content development and syndication services for organizations working with death and dying issues. The primary mission of Growth House is to improve the quality of compassionate care for people who are dying, through public education and global professional collaboration. Its search engine provides access to the Internet's most comprehensive collection of reviewed resources for end-of-life care.

Hospice Patients Alliance (HPA)
4541 Gemini St., PO Box 744, Rockford, MI 49341-0744
(616) 866-9127
e-mail: patientadvocates@hospicepatients.org
Web site: www.hospicepatients.org

The Hospice Patients Alliance was formed in August of 1998 as a non-profit charitable organization serving the general public throughout the United States. It was formed by experienced hospice staff and other health care professionals who saw that hospices were not always complying with standards of care. HPA provides information about hospice services; directly assists patients, families, and caregivers in resolving difficulties they may have with current hospice services; and promotes better quality hospice care throughout the United States.

International Task Force on Euthanasia and Assisted Suicide
PO Box 760, Steubenville, OH 43952
(740) 282-3810
Web site: www.internationaltaskforce.org

The task force opposes assisted suicide and euthanasia and strives to combat attitudes, programs, and policies that its members believe threaten the lives of those who are medically vulnerable. It supports the rights of people with disabilities, and advocates for the improvement of pain control for the seriously or terminally ill. The task force conducts seminars and workshops on euthanasia and related end-of-life issues. Its publications include pamphlets such as *Assisted Suicide: The Continuing Debate*, the book *Power over Pain: How to Get the Pain Control You Need*, and the periodic newsletter *Update*.

National Hospice and Palliative Care Organization (NHPCO)
1700 Diagonal Rd., Suite 625, Alexandria, VA 22314
(703) 837-1500 • fax: (703) 837-1233
e-mail: info@nhpco.org • Web site: www.nhpco.org

The NHPCO (originally the National Hospice Organization) was founded in 1978 to educate the public about the benefits of hospice care for the terminally ill and their families. It seeks to promote the idea that with the proper care and pain medication, the terminally ill can live out their lives comfortably and in the company of their families. The organization opposes euthanasia and assisted suicide. It conducts educational and training programs for administrators and caregivers in numerous aspects of hospice care. The NHPCO publishes grief and bereavement guides, brochures such as *Hospice Care: A Consumer's Guide to Selecting a Hospice Program* and *Communicating Your End-of-Life Wishes*, and the book *Hospice Care: A Celebration*.

Physicians for Compassionate Care Educational Foundation
PO Box 6042, Portland, OR 97228-6042
(503) 533-8154 • fax: (503) 533-0429
e-mail: stevensk@ohsu.edu • Web site: www.pccef.org

The Physicians for Compassionate Care Educational Foundation is an association of physicians and other health professionals dedicated to preserving the traditional relation of the physician and patient as one in which the physician's primary task is to heal the patient and to minimize pain. The foundation promotes the health and well-being of patients by encouraging physicians to comfort patients and to assist those who are dying by support systems, minimizing pain, and treating depression. The foundation affirms the health-restoring role of the physician and works to educate the profession and the public to the dangers of euthanasia and physician-assisted suicide.

Bibliography

Books

David Barnard et al.   *Crossing Over: Narratives of Palliative Care.* New York: Oxford University Press, 2000.

Alexander A. Bove   *The Complete Book of Wills, Estates, and Trusts.* New York: Henry Holt, 2000.

Kathryn L. Braun, James H. Pietsch, and Patricia L. Blanchette, eds.   *Cultural Issues in End-of-Life Decision Making.* Thousand Oaks, CA: Sage, 2000.

Clifton D. Bryant, ed.   *Handbook of Death and Dying.* Thousand Oaks, CA: Sage, 2003.

Grace Hyslop Christ   *Healing Children's Grief: Surviving a Parent's Death from Cancer.* New York: Oxford University Press, 2000.

William R. Clark   *A Means to an End: The Biological Basis of Aging and Death.* New York: Oxford University Press, 2002.

Mark Cobb   *The Dying Soul: Spiritual Care at the End of Life.* Philadelphia: Open University Press, 2001.

Raphael Cohen-Almagor   *The Right to Die with Dignity: An Argument in Ethics, Medicine, and Law.* Piscataway, NJ: Rutgers University Press, 2001.

Inge Corless, Barbara B. Germino, and Mary A. Pittman, eds.   *Dying, Death, and Bereavement: A Challenge for Living.* 2nd ed. New York: Springer, 2003.

Betty J. Eadie   *Embraced by the Light: Personal Triumphs over Loss and Grief.* Everett, WA: Ojinjinkta, 2002.

R.E. Erwin   *Reasons for the Fear of Death.* Lanham, MD: Rowman & Littlefield, 2002.

Kathleen Foley and Herbert Hendin, eds.   *The Case Against Assisted Suicide: For the Right to End of Life Care.* Baltimore: Johns Hopkins University Press, 2002.

Gregg Horowitz   *Sustaining Loss.* Palo Alto, CA: Stanford University Press, 2001.

Glennys Howarth and Oliver Leaman, eds.   *Encyclopedia of Death and Dying.* London and New York: Routledge, 2001.

John Keown   *Regulating Voluntary Euthanasia.* New York: Cambridge University Press, 2002.

Elisabeth Kübler-Ross	*The Tunnel and the Light: Essential Insights on Living and Dying.* New York: Marlow, 1999.
David Kuhl	*What Dying People Want: Practical Wisdom for the End of Life.* New York: Public Affairs, 2002.
Susan Lendrum and Gabrielle Syme	*Gift of Tears: A Practical Approach to Loss and Bereavement in Counseling and Psychotherapy.* 2nd ed. Philadelphia: Brunner-Routledge, 2004.
Erich H. Loewy and Roberta Springer Loewy	*The Ethics of Terminal Care: Orchestrating the End of Life.* New York: Kluwer Academic/Plenum, 2000.
Beverley McNamara	*Fragile Lives: Death, Dying and Care.* Philadelphia: Open University Press, 2001.
Jessica Mifford	*The American Way of Death Revisited.* New York: Vintage Books, 2000.
Ernest Morgan et al.	*Dealing Creatively with Death: A Manual of Death Education and Simple Burial.* Hinesburg, VT: Upper Access, 2001.
Barbara A. Olevitch	*Protecting Psychiatric Patients and Others from the Assisted-Suicide Movement: Insights and Strategies.* Westport, CT: Praeger, 2002.
Timothy E. Quill	*Caring for Patients at the End of Life: Facing an Uncertain Future Together.* New York: Oxford University Press, 2001.
Renee C. Rebman	*Euthanasia and the Right to Die: A Pro/Con Issue.* Berkeley Heights, NJ: Enslow, 2002.
Barbara Roberts	*Death Without Denial, Grief Without Apology: A Guide for Facing Death and Loss.* Troutdale, OR: NewSage Press, 2002.
Susy Smith	*Afterlife Codes: Searching for Evidence of the Survival of the Soul.* Charlottesville, VA: Hampton Roads, 2000.
Wesley J. Smith	*Culture of Death: The Assault on Medical Ethics in America.* San Francisco: Encounter Books, 2000.
Margaret A. Somerville	*Death Talk: The Case Against Euthanasia and Physician-Assisted Suicide.* Montreal: McGill-Queen's University Press, 2002.
Sue Woodman	*Last Rights: The Struggle over the Right to Die.* Cambridge, MA: Perseus, 2000.
Steven J. Zeitlin and Ilana Beth Harlow	*Giving a Voice to Sorrow: Personal Responses to Death and Mourning.* New York: Perigee Books, 2001.

Periodicals

| Mercedes Bern-Klug | "The Decision Labyrinth: Helping Families Find Their Way Through Funeral Options," *Generations*, Summer 2004. |

Bill Beuttler	"Mourning in America," *Boston Magazine*, November 2001.
B. Bower	"Good Grief: Bereaved Adjust Well Without Airing Emotion," *Science News*, March 2, 2002.
Consumer Reports on Health	"When to Ask About Hospice," January 2002.
Andrew J. DeMaio	"Drafting an Advance Directive for Health Care: Personal Reflections," *Estate Planning*, August 2002.
Julia Duin	"Avoiding Death: Americans Tend to Put Lives Ahead of the Inevitable," *Washington Times*, February 13, 2002.
Neil Genzlinger	"On Death, Life's Cruelest Lesson," *New York Times*, September 15, 2002.
August Gribbin	"Graceful Exit," *Washington Times*, January 7, 2001.
Jerome Groopman	"Dying Words," *New Yorker*, October 28, 2002.
E.M. Hollander	"Cyber Community in the Valley of the Shadow of Death," *Journal of Loss and Trauma*, 2001.
P.E. Kummervold et al.	"Social Support in a Wired World," *Nordic Journal of Psychiatry*, 2002.
Mark S. Lachs and Pamela Boyer	"Have This Discussion Now: 'My Mom's Friends Say She Should Make Out an Advance Directive. What Is That, and Does She Really Need to Have It?'" *Prevention*, March 2002.
Daniel E. Lee	"Physician-Assisted Suicide: A Conservative Critique of Intervention," *Hastings Center Report*, vol. 33, No. 1, 2003.
Charlotte Lobuono	"A Detailed Examination of Advance Directives," *Patient Care*, November 15, 2000.
Kathryn Jean Lopez	"Dr. Death Down Under," *Human Life Review*, Fall 2001.
Paul Malley	"Maintaining God-Given Dignity at the End of Life," *Clergy Journal*, February 2004.
Peter W. Marty	"A Different Kind of Funeral," *Christian Century*, October 17, 2001.
Lisa Miller	"Why We Need Heaven," *Newsweek*, August 12, 2002.
Joshua Mitteldoft	"Whence Comes Death?" *Humanist*, January/February 2002.
Janis Moody	"Dementia and Personhood: Implications for Advance Directives," *Nursing Older People*, June 2003.

National Right to Life News   "The Growing Trend Toward Involuntary Euthanasia," February 2001.

Emma Richler   "Two or Three Things I Know About Grief," *Maclean's*, June 24, 2002.

Pamela Roberts   "Here Today and Cyberspace Tomorrow: Memorials and Bereavement Support on the Web," *Generations*, Summer 2004.

Peter Singer   "Freedom and the Right to Die," *Free Inquiry*, Spring 2002.

W. St. John   "On the Final Journey, One Size Doesn't Fit All," *New York Times*, September 28, 2003.

Judith Timson   "Death Be Not Humble: Whatever Became of Simple Funerals?" *Chatelaine*, September 2002.

Tufts University Health and Nutrition Letter   "Making End-of-Life Medical Decisions Ahead of Time," September 2002. Available from 53 Park Pl., 8th Fl., New York, NY 10007.

Wendy Murray Zoba   "Dying in Peace," *Christianity Today*, October 22, 2001.

Index